FIRST COMES
COURAGE

LEADERSHIP STARTS WITHIN

SONIA MCDONALD

AUTHOR OF 'LEADERSHIP ATTITUDE' & 'JUST ROCK IT!'

Hardcover published in 2022 by Sonia McDonald
Paperback published in 2020 & re-published in 2021 by Sonia McDonald
Brisbane, Australia
www.soniamcdonald.com.au

Author: Sonia McDonald
Title: *First Comes Courage – Leadership Starts Within*
Hardcover ISBN: 9780994645265
Paperback ISBN: 9780994645234

Subjects: Leadership | Professional Development
Registered with the National Library of Australia
Book production services: smartwomenpublish.com

Disclaimer: The material in this publication is of the nature of general comment only and does not represent professional advice. All material is provided for educational purposes only. We recommend to always seek the advice of a qualified professional before making any decision regarding personal and business needs. To the maximum extent permitted by law, the author and publisher disclaim all responsibility and liability to any person arising directly or indirectly from any person taking or not taking action based on the information in this publication.

Other books published by Sonia McDonald

Leadership Attitude

Just Rock It!

CONTENTS

I dedicate this book to the most courageous person I know, my daughter Abby.

Sonia McDonald, author

ABOUT THE AUTHOR

Sonia McDonald is a dynamic and renowned speaker, author, entrepreneur, and founder of LeadershipHQ, McDonald Inc. and the Outstanding Leadership Awards.

With over 30 years professional experience, her mission is to empower people to move from good to great leadership. Sonia's passion is encouraging people to lead with courage, kindness, purpose, and impact.

Sonia achieves her passion by providing executive leadership coaching services, specialist consulting, and empowering keynote speaking on a range of topics including leadership, neuroscience, kindness, confidence, and courage. She is also championing great leaders and teams through the annual Outstanding Leadership Awards.

Her previous award-winning books - *Just Rock It!* and *Leadership Attitude* - are supported by a wide range of leadership materials that have been available globally.

Sonia's qualifications include a business degree majoring in human resources and psychology, as well as a diploma in neuroscience, combined with many years of professional experience in Australia and internationally.

Named one of the 'Top 250 Influential Women Across the Globe' by digital business magazine *Richtopia*, and one of the "Top 100 Australian Entrepreneurs', Sonia counts her role as a mother to her beautiful daughter, Abby above any other of her many achievements.

The inspiration behind this book is to build on the themes introduced in Sonia's previous books emphasising the importance of courage and kindness in our world today, as individuals, as members of our respective communities, and as leaders in business.

INTRODUCTION

'Courage is the most important of all the virtues, because without courage you can't practice any other virtue consistently. You can practice any virtue erratically, but nothing consistently without courage.'

MAYA ANGELOU, POET & CIVIL RIGHTS ACTIVIST

Understanding courage comes best through story telling!

A young martial arts student approached his teacher one day and asked him to show him how to be brave, how to be courageous and how to, one day, lead others with courage. The master focused his gaze intently on the young student for what seemed like an eternity, seemingly staring into his very soul. Finally, quietly and calmly he stated that he would teach the student on one condition; that for one month he must go into the city every day and tell every person he met that something good would happen in their day that day. The student must say it clearly and loudly and look directly into the person's eyes when he spoke to them.

For some people this would be an easy thing to do, but it really scared the young student. He was a quieter person, an introvert, and he felt he couldn't possibly complete the task. He mentally wrestled with it for days: he didn't understand why the teacher would ask him to do this before teaching him how to be courageous and brave. Had he gone completely crazy?

Finally, he decided to do it. What did he have to lose anyway? He summoned all his willpower and travelled into the city. He could hardly speak to the first person he met. He lost his words. His voice came out as barely a squeak. He mumbled the sentence half under his breath but managed to catch the eyes of the stranger as he did. The stranger did not look angry though; there was kindness in their eyes. The student took a little bit of confidence and courage from this.

This made it a little easier to speak to the next person he met, and he managed to catch their eyes and speak an audible, constructed sentence. As he continued with his task, his voice became louder, and his confidence grew. He was succeeding. His fear of speaking to strangers had not killed him; he had mastered it. When the task was finally complete, his fear had been replaced with courage.

This is a heart-warming story, but let's stop and think for a minute. What exactly is courage?

Courage has been defined as the ability to carry out acts that frighten us; to face extreme dangers or difficulties head on, seemingly without fear or concern for our own safety. It is placing ourselves directly in harm's way in order to help someone else. Courage is having a good belly laugh at danger, being strong in the belief that it can't beat us. We often hear the word courage used in the same breath as words like bravery, valour, daring or boldness.

Courage in action is harnessing the energy and fear that comes from uncertainty. In our story of the student, courage for him was moving forward into fear, doing what scared him, knowing, and believing that it would not beat him. Eventually fear went and courage was left in its place.

We can accomplish meaningful results from facing fear, by harnessing the resulting courage and plugging it into a higher purpose to create motivation and impact for positive change. This will drive continual development, and sustainable and ongoing advancement and improvement.

Courage and leadership must go hand in hand. Courageous leadership comes when we capitalise on the motivation we build once we harness fear and generate fortitude. Combine that with kindness and understanding to lead our teams, and we will inspire individuals within them to join us on this journey of discovery and growth. We have the opportunity to inspire courageous behaviours in our teams to deliver better results.

My thoughts on courageous behaviours and courageous leadership raise some potentially uncomfortable questions, though. Does courage exist without the presence of adversity? Do courage and adversity have the same integral relationship as fire does with oxygen? Is it possible that the fire of courage can't exist without the oxygen of adversity?

There is an argument that the true presence and strength of courage in our character is only tested through difficult circumstances or through our involvement in dangerous conditions—that it is only developed through multiple exposures to adversity and the ensuing perseverance required to overcome them.

In our roles as leaders of our teams, as parents, and as community members, we have to ask a question. If we say we have courage, but it has never been tested, are we potentially misleading others around us and causing damage to our personal reputation, our connections to others and our authenticity? In this situation, are we ultimately misleading ourselves? These are very valid points to ponder.

Where does courage come from? Is it an innate, instinctive behaviour or a learned behaviour that is developed over time?

An individual, whether they call themselves a leader or not, does not need to be, and in reality, may not be, a naturally courageous person. It may not be a characteristic that is present in their nature from birth. It may not be in their blood. It can be a frustrating thought when you hear that you 'either have it or you don't'.

But the good news is that courage is a trait that can be nurtured, developed, and grown with time. It can be built through experience, patience and endurance throughout our careers and our lives.

Courage is also reflective of our own personally held orientation, our values, and our focus. The way we demonstrate courage in our life shows whether we have an internal focus through self-driven motivation, or whether our motivation is driven by an external focus about others. It shows whether our own innate value sets place more importance on our own comfort and safety than on the lives of others. Or, alternately, whether we value other's safety or lives above our own.

This raises a set of philosophical questions, possibly rhetorical, but definitely worth discussion. These questions are pertinent in the context of leadership. Is it possible to have courage if we are internally focused? Is it a prerequisite to be externally focused, valuing other people's comfort, safety, and wellbeing over our own, in order to be courageous?

Interesting questions, aren't they? Throughout history, and in our everyday lives, we hear and see stories of courage and courageous people displaying extraordinary, selfless behaviours. Some of my favourite courage examples are:

- Fred Hollows, the eye specialist who treated the common eye disease, trachoma. Between 1974 and 1976 he helped over 100,000 Indigenous Australians living in remote areas to keep their sight. Following this, he turned his attention to treating the disease in Africa.

- Harriet Tubman, the American abolitionist, and political activist who led slaves to freedom through the Underground Railroad.
- Caroline Chisholm, who arrived in Australia in 1838 to find migrant women from Britain lying homeless and begging on the street. Over the next 10 years, she hounded bureaucrats and pestered the Governor to make conditions better for those arriving in the colony. She found housing and jobs for more than 10,000 women and girls.
- Martin Luther King Jr., the mouthpiece and leader of the Civil Rights Movement, who stood up for equal rights for his oppressed people.
- Mother Teresa, living amongst the poorest of the poor in her community in India, and touching over 133 other countries, helping underprivileged communities and individuals to thrive, learn and grow.
- The first responders, emergency workers and community members who helped those around them during the 2019/2020 Black Summer of severe bushfires in Australia.

These people and their stories highlight that fearlessness, tenacity and resilience are at the heart of courageous actions. But in today's largely self-centred, individualistic society, it is time we take a step back, capture a wide lens view and delve into the questions of the origin of courage and how it is fostered. We must consider its value in leadership and how we can build and grow it in our teams, in our communities and in our children. As we sometimes stride and sometimes stumble through the 21st century, our ability to lead with kindness and courage is critical in our fast-paced, high-pressured world.

What is the purpose of this book and why should you read on? This book is here to add commentary and promote an important discussion about the value and importance of courage and kindness in leadership. Through this book, together we will explore the power of courageous leadership and give you and your teams the insights and tools to develop, nurture and grow courage. It's an inspirational 'how to', showing you how to become courageous leaders, building and leading bold teams. I hope it will empower you to be spirited, confident, dauntless, selfless, and courageous in all aspects of your life.

Would you love that? I would love that for you. Let's start now. I'm excited for us to take this journey together. I'm excited to laugh with you, cry with you and support you through providing inspiration, provoking thought, and helping you to nurture and grow courage and kindness.

As a background, I am a motivational speaker, founder of LeadershipHQ (LHQ) and McDonald Inc. as well as the Outstanding Leadership Awards program, established in 2019. I am also an award-winning author and full-time solo mum. I mention these roles here because they all take a lot of courage to do well, especially the one that calls me to be the best parent I can be, in order to raise a courageous daughter who is resilient, confident and kind.

None of these roles were a part of my original pathway, none were a part of the plan I envisioned for my life. Not one. Well, that is not entirely true: I always wanted to be a mum, but I was told in my early twenties it would be incredibly challenging for me to have children. It devastated me then, but now I have my beautiful girl. However, I never expected the single mum role. The other roles and paths came out of nowhere and somewhere, and they are absolutely where I should be. But there is one constant in every path I have taken—each one has required courage, first and foremost.

Why did I write this book? I have been researching, writing, and speaking about courage and leadership for many years, but it had not occurred to me at the time to write a book focused on courage and how it relates to leadership. When I wrote my first book, *Leadership Attitude,* several years ago, I wrote a chapter on courage, but it was not something I felt the need to expand on. A few years later, in my second book, *Just Rock It!,* I did expand on this theme. I encouraged readers to be courageous and be brave. To rock your dreams and make them reality. To do this with courage, with resilience, with impact.

The foundation of this book was derived from a research trip to Japan a few years ago. Why Japan? I have had an enduring love affair with the country for a number of years. I knew the Japanese history and rich culture would give me an abundance of exceptional examples of courage, as well as kindness. As I had hoped, Japan did provide me with the inspiration and motivation to bring this book about courage to life. Naturally, there are many other inspirational people and cultures included in these pages as well, but that was my starting point.

Along my investigative journey, while connecting with hundreds of people to gain their insights on courage, it became very apparent that the research and data I was collecting wasn't restricted to just courage alone. It was also revealing adversity, heartache, fear, crises, challenge, and circumstances that brought out courage and courageous leadership. It became clear that courage was the drive to overcome difficult circumstances; to turn fear of uncertainty into motivation to achieve; to move through, to press on, showing resilience and determination.

It became clear that in order to foster courage, there needed to be fear, adversity and heartache. They are the ingredients that combine to deliver something truly beautiful: they deliver courage and courageous leadership.

I believe that these four attributes—kindness, impact, purpose, and resilience—are essential to courageous leadership. They determine a true leader's behaviour and guide them along the pathway of selfless and intrepid influence. They can also guide your journey of improvement as an individual, as a family member, as a community member, and as a leader.

As I am writing this in the midst of a global health crisis and a plethora of other difficult challenges that are playing out around the globe, I know it is even more important today than ever to harness fear. To act with purpose and impact. To act with kindness. To be kind to yourself. To be resilient. To see that first comes courage.

For easy reading, the book is summarised this way:

> Section 1: Courage Foundations
> Section 2: The Courage Compass™
> Section 3: Courage in Life
> Section 4: Leadership for the Future

The whole book is underpinned by the Courage Compass™ foundation.

The purpose of this book is to take you on your own courageous journey by looking at where you are today and then noting your own experiences through each chapter, which you can then summarise at the end. And, as we know, small actions accumulate into successful outcomes! Success breeds success.

To begin your journey, reflect on this chapter, check where you are in your own courageous journey, what your achievements and insights have been so far, and where you would like to be after reading this book.

- ....

- ....

- ....

- ....

- ....

*'You can be strong as a
leader and be kind.*

*You can be courageous as a
leader and be fearful.*

You can be a leader without the title.

But first comes courage.'

SONIA MCDONALD

COURAGE FOUNDATIONS

*'If you have built castles
in the air, your work need
not be lost; that is where
they should be. Now put the
foundations under them.'*

HENRY DAVID THOREAU, 'WALDEN'

MY 'FIRST COMES COURAGE' STORY

*'Courage is the main
quality of leadership, in
my opinion, no matter
where it is exercised.'*

WALT DISNEY, ENTREPRENEUR

Leadership is an attitude, a choice, and an action. It wasn't until I discovered the courage to lead that I realised this. And it wasn't until my world had taken a new and unexpected turn that I discovered my true courage. I am sure there had been a number of times where I was courageous early in my life, however courage does not shine it's brightest until it is shining in darkness which comes through adversity. Earlier in my life and my fledgling leadership career, I was more attached to safety and a level of certainty, to be honest. Don't we all feel like this to some degree? Isn't the goal of most people to settle, supported by certainty, and avoid difficulties where possible? It's just in us as humans. But nerve is not truly courage until it is tested.

It wasn't until I packed up my safe life here in Australia and moved overseas to China in my early 30s, with my then three-year-old daughter Abby and my husband, that I learned what true courage was. It was supposed to be an exciting time in our shared lives, a time with new beginnings, new adventures, and new discoveries. In reality, it turned out to be completely the opposite.

I knew the transition for my daughter and myself would be challenging. We had to assimilate into a new culture, meet new people and develop a new support base. However, it was much tougher and far more confronting than I had expected, even in my worst-case scenario.

After landing a dream role there in a senior position in a leading organisation and trying my best to settle my little girl into a new kindergarten, my life fell apart. It was so unexpected, and it hit me like a lightning bolt out of the clear blue sky.

I remember the day like it was yesterday, the day that changed my life. My husband decided to abandon my baby girl and me in Shanghai. He just left. No worthwhile explanation. No warning. No apology. Nothing.

Abby and I found ourselves alone in a foreign country, with very little money, no family, and no support base. Even though I had made friends there, I didn't have a strong network. I truly had to call on my courage.

One of my friends recommended I see a psychologist to help me process what had happened and help me work through and answer the many burning questions I had. Would I be okay? And most importantly, where, and how was I going to manage our lives in the immediate and more distant future?

I recall walking into her room, and her telling me to sit down in her strong American accent. I talked for an hour. I spoke about the impact the events had on us as a family. I spoke of my pain, my disbelief, and my fears for the future. I paid her $100 USD for the session and was preparing to leave. The psychologist had barely said a word up until this point, then she broke her silence. When she did, it was profound. The words she said then were a turning point in my journey and set me on my path of courage.

She said to me, 'See that door at the other side of the room? I want you to leave now, take your daughter, and get on a plane and go.' It was so unexpected. It was blunt. I was in shock.

She continued by saying that I needed to find the courage to go home, to go back to Australia and start again. She said staying in China as a single parent was not safe. It would not lead to the best future for me and my baby. She felt my husband could do the wrong thing by us and we would not be protected financially.

So, I left. It took only a few weeks to book a flight home and pack all we had. I got on the plane with Abby, and as she slept, I sobbed the whole flight home. I had to start again. Start a new life from nothing. It took inner courage. It took resilience, but we had to do it. We had to do it together. How did I survive? It took a clear mind and commitment to my goal. It took all my power, energy, and everything I had in me to overcome the roadblocks in my way. But we succeeded. Together.

But that was not the last time I have had to build backbone and show courageous leadership. There were other challenges waiting for us in our future. I discovered that there is no pain in a mother's world that is anything close to watching your child go through tough times. Abby was 13 years old when she started being bullied at school. For a long time, she didn't tell me. She turned to self-harming to release the pain she felt from others hurting her. She felt alone. She felt abandoned. She felt she was not enough—not valued or valuable as a person.

Her school did nothing! We contacted the police when it got out of control on social media, but it was out of their hands. They did nothing. We felt we had nowhere to turn. No one to help us. We were on our own. Her mental health issues became more difficult for her to manage, and she decided to leave school at 14. It was a dreadful and debilitating time for us both. I felt so lost and heartbroken for her.

I tried everything I could to help her, as any mother would. We were in and out of hospital so many times that I lost count. I didn't handle it well. I was also trying to run and grow my new company at the time, and I was dropping balls all over the place. Everywhere. At one time it was so difficult that I nearly lost both Abby and my company. It took all the courage I had within me, and more. There were days when I didn't know if I could do it. There were days I didn't want to be courageous, brave, or resilient. There were days I broke too, but I had to keep moving forward for her, one step at a time. I had to be courageous for both of us, to get us both through.

Today Abby and I continue to find the courage we need every day to keep moving forward with managing her mental health. Abby continues on with amazing tenacity and every day she gets stronger. She is by far the most courageous person I know. She tells me that for her, it's me, and I smile with tears of joy every time she says it. It is amazing when you love someone so much, how the courage you need is forged in steel.

Today she is at university studying social work and wants to build a career helping others. She began her tertiary studies at a Technical and Further Education (TAFE) institute at 15, as she had a dream to go to university and complete her PhD. This is a girl who left school at 14 due to bullying. But she had the courage to go back to study despite all her mental health issues, her fear of the unknown, and uncertainty about what was next for her. She passes every one of her subjects with flying colours and even her lecturers can't believe she left school when she was so young. She is absolutely the most valiant person I know. I have no doubt she will continue to grow into a strong, caring, courageous leader.

As indicated earlier, leadership is an attitude, a choice, and an action. The unexpected twists and turns in our lives and in our environments provide us with many opportunities to be courageous. To lead with spirit. To be courageous leaders.

The day I came home to Australia after living in China, I observed a cultural change in leadership in this country. Leadership, as I believe it should be, did not exist anymore. It had been replaced by leadership driven by popularity polls, not by impact or purpose. The change was evident in leadership thinking. It was obvious in leadership behaviour. And it impacted organisational behaviour. This lack of real leadership showed me how critically a workforce can be impacted by poor leadership standards.

Leadership, as a word, was on everyone's lips. Its theory was at the forefront in everyone's minds. But this wasn't true leadership I was seeing. Yes, it was leading by challenging—challenging to innovate, challenging to collaborate, challenging to experiment and deliver better results. It was efficiency and profit-focused; it was about leading with the intention of risking more for a higher reward.

These objectives can bring results; they can be driven by a growth mindset of continual increase and improvement. But they also can lead in the wrong direction.

That form of management was really about practising leadership without any regard or consideration that their followers are people who have their own individual needs. It was leading without an understanding of why people follow good leaders. It was definitely not authentic leadership; it was not courageous leadership. It was not leadership guided by kindness, impact, purpose, and resilience. It was a thin shadow of what leadership should be, its impact neither tangible nor durable.

So, in summary, what are the essential ingredients needed for courage to grow and drive leadership? In order to see you through adverse times and give those around you a sense of security and safety, you need a robustness or toughness of character, a resolve to stand strong and a courageous mindset.

Toughness has quite a subjective definition, though. I've seen people who value toughness above all else, actually struggle to adapt when a situation calls for a softer style. An approach that is steadfast but still flexible is required.

I believe kindness is critical when it comes to courage in leadership, as you can still be strong as a leader, still be steadfast, while being flexible and understanding through kindness. Kindness supports an external focus in a leader. A kind leader is more focused on the wellbeing of others and their teams than their own success. In this way, kindness supports courage in leadership.

Many agree that kindness in leadership is defined by attributes such as humility, authenticity, integrity, compassion, and gratitude. Many times, people who exhibit these traits are the most likely to be respected as formal or informal leaders. They become natural leaders, potentially without the title or trappings.

> There are many examples of kind leaders available to us, some of which we have mentioned already. The actions of Mother Theresa and Harriet Tubman were based purely in kindness. These amazing ladies worked tirelessly, with purpose and with impact, and a selflessness that allowed their leadership strength to shine through. This approach inspired people to follow in their footsteps. To buy into their vision. A vision that was delivered with a kindness, toughness and tenacity that allowed them to achieve results.

What about showing no fear? After all, if courage is the ability to carry out acts that frighten us, courage in action is harnessing the fear of uncertainty and using it with purpose and impact to drive motivation for change.

Courage is fear … it is the method for mastering fear. I believe this with every fibre of my being. It is why I love to use the word 'resilience' when describing true leadership. The best leaders embrace the fear, and with strength, tenacity, kindness, and a growth mindset they identify improvements and move forward.

In addition, knowledge, intelligence, toughness, hard work, self-lessness—these qualities and others—are important components of leadership. In varying quantities, they are foundational. But above every other quality of leadership, courage is the one that separates real leaders from people who simply have the titles and trappings of authority.

> *Courage is not peeking around the corner with one eye on the calculator, trying to figure out when the odds are safest for you to step out and say something.*
> *Courage isn't playing it safe.*
> *Courage isn't managing risk.*
> *Courage isn't a science experiment.*
> *Courage isn't working the odds.*
> *Courage isn't putting yourself first, always.*
> *Courage isn't a statement from your spokesperson.*
> *Courage isn't putting someone down.*

So, what is courage in leadership? And why should it come first?

Courage is stepping up and standing out—often by yourself—when you know something needs to be said.

Courage is leaping before you look, in the name of a greater good.

Courage can be lonely and scary.

Courage is making an impact and leaving a legacy.

Courage is knowing why you do what you do.

Courage requires thick skin and resilience.

Courage is about being strong as well as kind.

Courage is being able to proudly tell your kids and grandkids that you didn't wait for someone else's permission, or the math to add up in your favour, before you stood up for what you believed in.

Courage requires you to have something to lose, and the willingness to potentially lose it for the wider good, or the good of someone else.

Courage allows you to develop with a growth mindset. To seek out improvement opportunities and implement them to make you a better person, a better parent, a better leader.

What about insight, one of the most important proficiencies we can develop on our journey of growth and courage as a human being? Gaining insight will give you new perspectives; it will give you balance in living and leading. It will allow you to become a courageous and insightful leader, responding to your environment appropriately and with maximum impact.

Insight allows us to look deeper, beyond the apparent to what is really happening behind the scenes. To illustrate, consider a regular morning commute where you observe that the traffic is particularly heavy. Your insight may be that as humans, we are creatures of habit. We will often endure something uncomfortable (like a long commute) rather than change the way we do things (like changing travel times or routes, or even jobs). It takes courage to change the way we do things; it takes a growth mindset to consider, deliver and accept positive change. It takes strong insight. Through insight we can imagine then deliver change that is meaningful and makes our world a better place.

In your leadership journey, no matter where you are on your path, courage is the underlying attribute that will enable you, drive you, and inspire you. A growth mindset shows you areas of improvement. Insight supports the application of courage in the world around you.

But first comes courage.

———————————

Write down 5 insights and actions that stand out for you in this chapter:

- ....

- ....

- ....

- ....

- ....

Courageous Thoughts

Leadership is an attitude and a mindset
that lead to an action.

The potential for leadership is
everywhere, and within all of us.

There are many quasi-leadership styles in our
world today, but true, authentic leadership is
based solely on courage and a growth mindset
to seek out opportunities for improvement.

FIRST COMES COURAGE FOR YOU

'Courage is the first of human qualities because it is the quality which guarantees the others.'

ARISTOTLE

L eadership is everywhere, but why do we still struggle with it? Can it really be that we still see leadership only as a role or title? To reflect on your own courageous journey, it's important to look at examples of leadership where things could have been done more effectively.

It has been said that the only thing leaders need are followers. This points to something bigger than title or role. I wondered if true leadership is more than this though. More than just having followers. Why do leaders have followers at all? What draws people to follow them?

To enhance your perspectives on courageous leadership, I am including different views and examples for reflection.

A young leader in an organisation had a particularly difficult team member who was incredibly averse to change. The team member's attitude was evident in his private life as well as his work life. He refused to engage in team building exercises. He refused to be part of the team and work as a team contributor. He was negative and everyone walked on eggshells around him.

The young leader had no option but to address the team member's attitude and call him out on his behaviour. In addition, if the team member decided to change his behaviour at work, he would need the young leader's support. He would also need the professional development resources and tools available to him through the organisation to help him improve performance.

Unfortunately, the young leader's demeanour and approach were timid. He was not yet confident in his leadership abilities and was no match for the team member's set-in-stone, overbearing approach. While the young leader had the job title, he lacked courage. It was not something that come naturally to him. It needed to be built, to be seeded and nurtured. The young man was not yet a leader. He did not yet have the right tools, the right motivation, the right attitude, the right mindset to guide others.

While researching and writing my first book, *Leadership Attitude,* I experienced an epiphany. I discovered that leadership is having an attitude and a mindset that lead to an action. Therefore, the potential for leadership is everywhere, and within us all. Yes, it sometimes needs to be nurtured and developed, but it is there. It just takes focus, a growth mindset and intention.

It takes courage to embrace the challenge, to convert potential leadership to reality by bringing it to the forefront and nurturing it into its full capacity. Courage itself—particularly courage of this magnitude—is not always an innate behaviour in us humans. It's not necessarily present in our characters from birth. It is something that may itself need developing before it can be used to unlock the leadership potential in all of us.

Reflecting on the example I shared:

> The young leader sought out a strong mentor, and through focused personal development activities over time, he embraced fear, building courage and confidence which impacted his leadership style and capabilities. He did this through role-plays, learning from his mentor, targeted training and confronting his fears. He was introduced to new principles and practised being guided by kindness, leading with courage and purpose, delivering impact, and showing resilience.

With these tools, the young leader built the courage to finally address the situation with his renegade team member. Although it was a tough conversation, and it was delivered with kindness, the team member became agitated and walked out of the meeting after all of the concerns were laid out for discussion.

But the young leader had actually addressed the issue, and with stunning results. Within an hour, the team member returned to the young leader's office to thank him for having the courage to speak with him. He then sought help and gradually, as he overcame his own fears and built the courage to change, his behaviours improved. The young leader had to build courage in his leadership to succeed, to become a true leader, not just a leader by title.

This summary of change in the young leader illustrates that leadership is truly in all of us. While courage may not be born in us, we can build it with the help of a growth mindset. And that's a good thing, because every time we read or hear a story of less-than-good leadership, we are reminded that the title of 'leader' alone is not enough.

What are some other relatable and unfortunate leadership-without-courage moments that have been exhibited by leaders with all the titles and trappings? I've picked out two to highlight my point.

Theranos was a start-up company that sought to disrupt the lucrative world of health care. The leadership team aimed to do this by building an alternative to traditional blood testing that was cheaper for the medical health system and less invasive for the patient. This had all the hall markings of a situation that required a leadership team who would lead with kindness, impact, purpose, and resilience; leadership that was willing to take on the establishment and make things better for those who are unwell.

What went so wrong for the Theranos leadership team?

> An investigative report by the Wall Street Journal questioned some of the company's linchpin claims about process and methods. For a founder and leadership team, this was an opportunity to stand out and lead with courage and gusto. However, while the business's testing and methods were bravely defended, the team did not display the courage to allow independent scrutiny of their internal procedures. Not having the courage to face the potential growth opportunities and improvements in processes that might be identified in the independent examination resulted in federal regulators losing faith in the Theranos labs. The regulators found that there were serious deficiencies that posed an immediate risk to patient health and safety. The start-up at that point was defunct.

If the leadership team had had the courage to face the independent investigation, and back their staff, labs, and processes, they may have delivered a different result. By embracing the opportunity given to them to improve, with a growth mindset, the situation may have ended very differently.

My second example of leadership-with-all-the-trappings-but-without-courage moments is the CEO and leadership team of Volkswagen.

> These were leaders who were asleep at the wheel—figuratively speaking, of course—when VW engineers were installing software in vehicles that allowed them to effectively manipulate results when testing emission levels in the cars. The 'cheat' impacted approximately 11 million vehicles worldwide and tarnished the reputation of a strong brand. Worldwide!

However, this situation alone does not win the Volkswagen leadership team a place on my list of non-courageous leaders. What confirmed their position was the fact that, collectively, they did not display the courage to own up to what had happened and take responsibility for it. The CEO pled ignorance, even though he was widely known as a micro-manager who was notorious for being involved in the detail of the business. He was not courageous enough to admit there was a problem and, with his team, lead his people through it to a resolution. He was not leading with a continuously improving growth mindset.

Digressing for a moment, I want to argue that micro-management is not leadership in the true sense of the word, either. Micro-management does not lead people through adversity to overcome their fear, to grow as humans and achieve a higher plane in their development. No, I propose that style of management drives people to achieve outcomes that may or may not be helpful to them. It does not build their own courage or confidence; it simply delivers exactly what someone else orders, without variation. It does not inspire teams or individuals through courage, kindness, and integrity. It uses either a carrot or a stick model to achieve a specific result. It stifles innovation and personal empowerment. (I will now hop down off my soap box and return to the topic at hand.)

Looking at the examples of non-courageous leadership provided above, we are reminded that true and courageous leadership is in short supply. Perhaps this is because we talk a lot about leadership, but not enough about the characteristics, traits and actions that make a courageous leader.

Leadership, after all, is the fruit of the tree, not the tree itself.

I often question what separates the leadership teams of Thernaos or Volkswagen from leaders of great calibre, such as Caroline Chisholm and Winston Churchill, and others of such ilk. The key point, I have decided, is courage—the courage to step up, take responsibility and take control. That type of courage gives people a perception of safety and security. If people see this and feel safe that you, as their leader, are willing and able to take on an adverse situation and guide them through it to help them not only survive, but grow and develop as a result, they will naturally follow you.

Courage provides stable, trustworthy roots for the leadership tree. But how often do you see discussion that focuses on courage, or attempts to define courage?

Far too little, I feel. That's disappointing because we need courageous leadership more today than ever before, with our world constantly going through change, crisis, and disruption. That type of leadership will give people the confidence to follow and act as well. It may not reduce the complexity of the situation, but it will model resilience and action, which will help people see the adversity through, and learn and grow from a tough situation. But first comes courage.

Of course, you might ask, what about knowledge, technical skills, and intelligence? Courage is all very well, but aren't they important too?

Those qualities matter, but no one can dispute that a lot of technically brilliant and clever people have failed as leaders. Knowing and doing can be vastly different things. The examples of leadership without courage that we discussed above tell us this. There is no doubt in my mind that leaders such as Holmes (founder and CEO of Theranos) and Winterkorn (CEO of Volkswagen) are very intelligent, knowledgeable, and educated people. Their failure as leaders is no reflection on their intellectual ability, training, or technical skill.

What about being a hard worker? Will being committed to your goal and delivering it make you a good leader?

In a word, my answer is no. Sure, committing yourself fully to the cause is essential. That's what gives you purpose. But it's not everything. I've been around individuals who defined leadership as the willingness to work 40 hours in a 24-hour day. Unfortunately, this approach isn't conducive to anyone's mental, physical, or emotional health or well-being. I've seen it many times. It's an unsustainable approach that drains the energy from everyone involved. It fails to inspire those who hope to follow that leader.

In place of hard work, I prefer the words 'impact' and 'purpose' to define a high-achieving leadership style. I want to lead where we all work hard for a purpose—to deliver a positive and sustainable impact. I don't mean the '40 hours in a 24-hour day' approach. I mean we work and lead together, in a sustainable and healthy way, to deliver impact based on a clear and meaningful purpose.

> I recall a former manager of mine who worked an untenable schedule. Despite the hard work, she seemed to have no purpose or impact. Very early on in our relationship, I concluded that I wanted to be nothing like her. Unfortunately, this inevitably lessened her influence on me and her power as a leader. And it meant that as a leader, she was not leading through example. No one in their right mind wanted to follow her precedent.

Write down 5 insights and actions you have gained from this chapter by reflecting on the examples and general thoughts on courageous leadership:

- ....

- ....

- ....

- ....

- ....

Courageous Thoughts

It takes courage to embrace challenge
and you have the ability to do that.

You can convert potential leadership to reality by bringing
it to the forefront and nurturing it into its full capacity.

COURAGEOUS MINDSET

'You gain strength, courage and confidence by every experience in which you really stop to look fear in the face. You are able to say to yourself, "I have lived through this horror. I can take the next thing that comes along". You must do the thing you think you cannot do.'

ELEANOR ROOSEVELT

I've woven a thread through earlier chapters that I think deserves further exploration—courageous mindset. It's the enabler of the Courage Compass™, explored later in this book, and an absolute must as we develop ourselves as courageous leaders. It's underpinned by a 'growth mindset' as opposed to a 'fixed mindset'. Being willing to tackle tough conversations. Being willing to fail and learn. Being willing to face things head on and succeed. Not telling ourselves that we can't; but leading our teams through to success.

Let's start with an example to understand what a courageous mindset looks like. I'm sure you have heard of well-known author, JK Rowling. In her life, Rowling consistently showed perseverance, courage, and fearlessness in the face of poverty, in the face of divorce, in the face of raising a child as a single parent, and in the face of losing her closest family member, mentor and fan—her mother. She continuously faces challenging interactions with the press; and she has also faced issues in her professional life, including working through difficulties faced through her businesses. But she faces all of these situations with courage. Seemingly without fear. She tackles them head on.

While it's inspirational to see courageous behaviours such as Rowling's, I have to wonder, what actually is a courageous mindset?

A courageous mindset is a way of thinking and driving behaviours that allows a willingness to adapt to changes. In the words of William Faulkner, '*you cannot swim for new horizons until you have courage to lose sight of the shore*'. This is the attitude that underpins a courageous mindset, no matter whether the changes are for the better, or if they appear to be for the worse. It's an essential outlook that uses creativity, intelligence, resilience, and courage to achieve what might seem like the impossible. It's taking us out of our comfort zones, forcing us to stop playing safe, and delivering success in areas that we would not have dreamed possible.

Being a leader with a courageous mindset makes you an unstoppable force, and that makes you irresistible to follow.

Now that we've seen courageous a mindset in action, and understand what it is, the next question is, how do you build a courageous mindset? Here are some ways to do that:

CHECK YOUR FOCUS

We've established that a courageous and kind mindset needs an external focus. Its basis is being aware of and prioritising the needs of others over our own. But there is also a paradox involved. In order to prioritise others and deliver the most value to them, we, as leaders, need to also have a level of internal focus. It is the courage to be kind to ourselves. To recognise that while our main concentration needs to be external, on others, we need to care for ourselves at the same time in order to deliver optimal value, We must take time to ensure our own batteries remain charged. As the well-known saying goes, you can't pour from an empty cup!

CLARIFY GOALS AND OBJECTIVES

To begin, it's important to establish priorities and clarify objectives and goals. These are your true north points, the things that you must never lose sight of, regardless of the twists and turns in the journey.

BELIEVE IN YOURSELF

Once your goals, objectives and priorities are set, you need to build an unshakable belief in these and in yourself to achieve them. That is, no matter what happens or what is thrown at you, you can work through it with a cool, calm head, drawing on your resilience and finding a way to deliver your goals.

Some experts call these identity-based habits. Habits that reflect exactly who you are, and that are driven by your self-belief. It's a non-negotiable: as individuals we have to believe we can achieve great things, without limits, if we are actually going to achieve them. This will build confidence as a person. It will build confidence as a leader. If we believe in ourselves. If we are thoroughly convinced that no matter what happens we are capable, able, and competent to achieve our goals, others will buy into these also. It's contagious.

DON'T WORRY, BE HAPPY

This is easily said, but more difficult in practice. A critical contribution to building our courageous mindsets is keeping those nagging worries at bay. Keep perspective. Worry keeps you in a highly alert state, which encourages fear and clouds your thinking. So, do whatever it takes for you to avoid worry. Meditate. Exercise. Distract yourself. Acknowledge the worst-case scenario and build a plan to work through it, should it happen. Understand what the likelihood of the worst-case scenario you are worrying about eventuating actually is. It's often said that about 96% of situations that we worry about, never actually eventuate. But that doesn't mean you can't be prepared. This will put your mind at rest and help you maintain a positive, open-minded attitude.

Positivity in this space is key. A positive mindset looks at what could be. It assumes that a good outcome is a pre-determined outcome: it's just how it is achieved that is in question. Optimism and positivity are core skills in your courageous mindset toolkit.

DECIDE THE KIND OF PERSON OR LEADER YOU WANT TO BE

Deciding who we want to be as people, as leaders, determines the path we take and the results we achieve. Reconfirming values, and how they will deliver goals and objectives is the first step. Being clear about this will focus your energy and attention, and ultimately deliver the goals that were set.

GET OUT OF YOUR COMFORT ZONE

There's danger in staying in our comfort zones. There is little to no growth here. We have to branch out and make ourselves uncomfortable to grow. I once heard someone say that 'you can choose courage, or you can choose comfort; what you can't do is choose both'. I believe this. Courage is grown through adversity, through discomfort. It's what gets us through the tough times. I've experienced it in my life. I've seen it play out in other people's lives.

BE OPEN TO GROWTH

As courageous people, courageous parents, courageous leaders, we need to accept that things will not always go our way. And when they don't, be brave enough to ask for feedback from your team, or from someone you trust. Be courageous enough to accept the opportunity to try another tack or to use an opportunity to grow. Be flexible enough to change your pathway, to course correct, while still keeping an eye on your goal.

Celebrate the steps you take on your journey. Celebrate the small wins. It's a marathon, not a sprint. Celebrate the things that have gone right. Remember, we are in it for the long haul, and change can take time. But if we celebrate the small wins, the big wins, and the waypoints on our journey, the result will be a sustainable and long-term courageous mindset. That drives strong leadership.

A chance to develop a courageous mindset in my own life came when I published my book, *Leadership Attitude*. While publishing that book, to be totally honest, I was scared shitless! So much so that it took a significant amount of time longer to publish than I had intended. After another delay in the writing and publishing process, I realised that it was my mindset that was holding me back. I was not open to growth; I did not have the belief in myself that would drive my success. I acknowledged that I needed to practise a courageous mindset that would ultimately drive courageous actions to underpin the way I went about things.

How did I do this? What did I do practically to change my mindset and behaviours? I visualised my book on the shelves of stores, with customers browsing, picking it up and enjoying what I had written. I visualised it being available on Amazon, being searched by leaders who were looking for a new way of leading. Who were looking to grow themselves. And I was right there helping them via my book.

This exercise showed me how I could make an impact on others. The value I could share with them. This gave me a courageous mindset and drove me to act with courage. It was a conscious choice I had to make. To take on this mindset. To move out of my comfort zone and lead with purpose, with impact, with kindness, with courage, with a courageous mindset.

We can choose to move ourselves away from comfort and adopt courage. It's a choice that I would like to encourage you to take with me. Make a conscious choice that will drive action. Work with me to build a courageous mindset you can rely on when needed.

Write down 5 insights and actions drawn from this chapter about your own courageous mindset and what you can change:

- ....

- ....

- ....

- ....

- ....

Courageous Thoughts

Being willing to face things head on and you will succeed.

Make a conscious choice that will drive
action through a courageous mindset.

COURAGEOUS LEADERSHIP

'A leader takes people where they want to go. A great leader takes people where they don't necessarily want to go, but ought to be.'

ROSALYNN CARTER

Greek philosopher, Heraclitus once said: '*Change is the only constant in life*'. In today's world of endless technological advancements, globalisation, uncertainty and seemingly endless crises, this sentiment is even more apt. Today we are crying out for leaders who can adapt to change and challenges. Leaders who can build partnerships with trust and integrity and use these to drive results. Leaders who have the courage to act and react in the face of challenges and inspire a workforce to follow them on what is sometimes an unknown journey.

What is it that sets this calibre of leadership apart? It's a question that has been debated at length by leadership experts and academics alike, and there are many diverse trains of thought. Is it transformational leadership tactics, a growth mindset focus, or the dreaded 'A' or 'MM' styles? (That's 'authoritarian' or 'micro-management': I hear you groan, and I can barely say the words myself.)

Fortunately, it has now been proven that authoritarian or micro-management styles rarely, if ever, deliver the lasting results in performance and development that businesses need. In fact, consistent micro-management is a major contributor to costly disengagement in the workplace, according to Harvard Medical School instructor Jonathan D. Quick, who co-authored a book titled *Preventive Stress Management in Organizations*.

So, let's look more closely at some other styles that deliver high calibre leaders:

1. First is transformational leadership. From all I have studied and seen in operation in organisations, transformational leadership is inspiring, it's fast paced, and it is focused on delivering results.

2. Second is growth mindset leadership. A growth mindset is critical to adaptation and survival. It means that leaders and individuals seek out opportunities for improvement in their own development and performance. It also fosters acceptance of change and delivers lasting results and continual improvement.

   Satya Nadella, CEO of Microsoft, embodies a growth mindset for the 100000+ people he manages. When Nadella took over Microsoft in 2014, he created change by pushing people to think of themselves as students. His view is that the 'learn-it-all' does better than the 'know-it-all'.

I have come to the conclusion, though, that while these leadership styles and attributes are incredibly important, courage is the one quality of leadership that separates real leaders from people with just the titles and trimmings of command.

In my first book, *Leadership Attitude*, I explored how the attitude of leadership can influence you, your style, and your success as a leader; how a mindset of courage and action can change your world. You can be strong as a leader, and kind. You can be courageous as a leader. You can be fearful. You can be a leader without the title.

It's a premise that flies in the face of many theories and approaches to leadership development in recent years. It is controversial. It is challenging.

To support a change in leadership thinking and approach today, forward-thinking leaders need examples to light the pathway for others on their journey. Stories they can relate to. Anecdotes to show them the way.

With this thought in mind, there is no better illustration of pure courageous leadership—without the title, without the showy trappings—than a story I found on my research trip to Japan.

Japan is a country very close to my heart, and its culture provides endless stories and examples of courageous leadership, with some formal leaders and many informal leaders doing extraordinary things in their day-to-day lives. This is a story I found when I was spending some time in a war museum that recorded history relating to World War Two. The story is of Tame Okada.

> Tame and her husband Kazuichi owned a successful haberdashery store, not far from the city of Hiroshima, Japan. In February of 1946, the couple were overjoyed at the safe birth of their son, Yoshikazu. The previous six months had been a struggle in the aftermath of the world's first atomic bomb dropped on Hiroshima in August 1945. Yoshikazu was the ray of light and happiness the family needed in a bleak time.

> Unfortunately, Tame had been exposed to the high level of radiation in the aftermath of the bomb. This level of exposure early in her pregnancy meant that baby Yoshikazu suffered mental, developmental, and learning disorders. His parents found out about these disabilities when he started nursery school. Due to their continuing effects, Yoshikazu was not able to keep pace with his peers in his learning and formal education. Yoshikazu's issues became more evident when he entered elementary school, where he struggled to grasp even the basics at the same pace as his classmates.

> Tame and Kazuichi realised this and bravely came up with a solution. Kazuichi built partnerships and connections in the Japanese education sector, and successfully used them to

drive adaptation and change in the very traditional system. He successfully worked to have the school that Yoshikazu attended provide separate classes tailored to Yoshikazu's special needs and those of other children with similar problems. Kazuichi also successfully worked later to have the same approach to classes and learning available in Yoshikazu's junior high school. Yoshikazu started to thrive under this specialised program and things started looking up once again.

But courage is not courage without adversity, and courageous leadership is not real without being tested. The Okada family certainly experienced their share of testing and more. As also happened to many people in the aftermath of the Hiroshima bomb, Kazuichi fell ill and died not long after he had successfully led the change in education for children with special needs in Japan. A devastated Tame was left alone to courageously carry on the work of her husband, continue earning an income through their family business and raise a child with special needs. But the adversity in Tame's life, and the opportunity to display courageous behaviours and lead with courage, was not over yet. Shortly after her husband died, their haberdashery store burned down in a fire that started in a neighbouring house.

That would have been enough to drive even the strongest person to despair. But not Tame. And this is where my deep respect and admiration for her developed.

Our courageous leader picked herself up, rebuilt the store and continued to raise Yoshikazu as a single parent. But Tame did not stop there. She also continued to lead the work her husband had started; the work in ensuring that their son, and many children just like him, had the opportunities they deserved to excel and thrive through nurturing, caring and tailored education.

Although not a world-renowned leader, or even a leader with a title, I feel Tame demonstrates the true abilities of a strong, courageous leader. She was obviously guided by courage, kindness, impact, purpose, and resilience. She also acted with unbelievable selflessness. She adapted to her situation and made the most of opportunities to grow and improve. She delivered results that changed the lives of many young people just like her son. She continually grew, developed, changed, and adapted to meet her new environment and the new challenges in her path.

While she had no formal leadership training, Tame used ingenuity and the tools she had at hand to continue her journey with toughness, with inventiveness, with purpose and with commitment. She had a mind that was open to improvement opportunities. She was open to change and could negotiate her way through it. She met all challenges that came her way head on. She reacted and adapted her approach when life threw her overwhelming curveballs and trials.

Both Tame and her late husband, Kazuichi, built trusting partnerships with schools to drive change. Following the death of her husband, Tame embraced action in the face of fear. Fear of loss. Fear of destitution. Fear for the wellbeing of her son. Fear of being a single parent to a child with special needs. She used this fear as motivation to drive her to success. She rebuilt her business. She continued her husband's legacy. She built a successful life for herself and her son.

Tame became a truly great leader, delivering life-changing impacts to those around her. A leader who adapted to new challenges: who built strategic partnerships, sustained human capital and who had the courage to act and react to the challenges that came her way.

This is truly courageous leadership.

Write down 5 insights and actions from this chapter about courageous leadership:

- ....

- ....

- ....

- ....

- ....

Courageous Thoughts

In today's world we are crying out for leaders who
can adapt to change and challenges, who can build
partnerships with trust and integrity, who have the courage
to act and react in the face of challenges, who inspire
a workforce to follow them on an unknown journey.

Courage and courageous leadership are not without
adversity; courageous leadership is not real without
being tested. True courageous leaders do not hide
from being tested, they react and act in the face of
challenge, inspiring their followers through their courage,
their kindness, their impact, and their purpose.

FACING FEAR

'Courage is resistance to fear, the mastery of fear, not the absence of fear.'

MARK TWAIN, WRITER & ENTREPRENEUR

Courage is fear. Courageous leaders face fear head on and lead those around them to deliver results.

The following story brought tears to my eyes and filled me with admiration for this amazing family and the courageous leadership they each showed.

Rukhsana Kausar was a 21-year-old woman who lived with her parents, Noor Hussain and Rashida Begum, and her 19-year-old brother, Aijaz. The family lived on a farm in the province of Jammu, India. Being close to the India–Pakistan border, the family had lived with military unrest in and around their town for many years. However, the ferocity of the unrest had reached alarming new levels in the months leading up to this incident.

On Sunday, 27 September 2009, at around 9:30 pm, three men from the Laskar-E-Taiba militants came to the house of Waqalat Hussain, Rukhsana's uncle. The militants demanded that Waqalat lead them to Rukhsana's house, on threat of violence, torture and death.

This was not an easy decision for Waqalat, as just a few months before in July, Rukhsana had been abducted by local youths, but later released without physical harm. The family were on high alert and definitely did not want a repeat of the abduction.

Being on his own at that point in time, and without any option to fight the militants, Waqalat reluctantly lead them to Noor's house, causing as much commotion as possible along the way. On hearing the noise, Noor did not respond to the militant's pounding on his door. He and his wife hid Rukhsana and her brother under a bed in a back bedroom to keep them safe. The parents then prepared themselves to fight and defend their little family.

The pounding on the door stopped momentarily but was immediately followed by the chilling sound of glass shattering. The militants had broken a window and entered the house using force. They demanded that Rukhsana be handed over to become the wife of the Commander of the group.

Rukhsana's parents and uncle tried to resist the militants but were severely beaten. One of the militants even opened fire, shooting Waqalat in his arm. It was at this point that Rukhsana decided it was time she and her brother acted. Rukhsana quickly briefed her brother on the plan she had in mind.

They found an axe that had been hidden with them in their hiding place and prepared for action. The duo charged from their hiding place with the axe, surprising the militants and allowing Rukhsana enough time to land a heavy blow on the head of the leader of the group, knocking him out cold.

Running on pure adrenaline and instinct, Rukhsana grabbed the Commander's AK47 assault rifle as it clattered to the floor. Rukhsana had never held a rifle in her life, and she had definitely never shot one. But this did not stop her. She led a coordinated charge with her brother, shooting and killing the Commander and making the other two militants flee for their lives. Rukhsana and her brother then led their family to the Shahdra Shareif Police Post and handed over the weapons.

As a result of these heroic actions, both Rukhsana and her brother Aijaz were awarded the India National Bravery Award. In the face of unbelievable fear, Rukhsana was driven to be a courageous leader. It was the resistance to fear and the mastery of fear that drove her, not the absence of fear. Fear for her life and her family's lives drove her to act in a way that she had never acted before, leading her brother with the skill of a seasoned commander. Fear did not impede Rukhsana from reaching her leadership potential; it drove her to become a strong and fearless leader.

So, what is fear? Fear is a basic human mechanism. It's an instinct built to help us survive. If something scares us, fear drives us to practice behaviours that will help us avoid that danger, now and in the future. When we successfully avoid that danger, we then feel rewarded.

Courage is mastering fear—not letting it hold us back but using it instead to drive us to do amazing things. The mastery of fear is the mark of a true leader. Reward comes when we master fear and conquer danger. But mastering fear does not always come naturally to us. It is not always an innate part of our character or nature. It is a trait that sometimes needs nurturing to reach its full potential.

Are you mastering fear in your leadership? Is fear impacting your leadership, your life, your business? Does a fear-based culture exist in your workplace? Traditionally, cultures of fear and punishment in organisations have been all too common. And these have long been proven to be stunningly ineffective. Rather than motivating a team to drive positive behaviours, fear and its contagion can drive undesirable and demotivating behaviours. From my experience, even the calmest, most even-tempered and unexcitable of personalities can be quickly drawn into a fight-or-flight reaction if they are being led under the tyranny of fear. This is definitely not helpful, not healthy and not supportive of worthwhile change.

Leaders today need to create team climates that drive positive action and allow members to respond to difficult challenges in ways that are productive and healthy, not driven by fear. These teams are able to let go of the fear of failure, the fear of change and the fear of taking risks. In doing this, they master fear and harness the energy for use in positive ways.

How can you face your own fear? Before we can tackle fear and let go of it, we firstly need to understand where it is coming from. Is it being driven from within the organisation or external to it? Is it uncertainty caused by organisational changes such as expansion, entering new territories or restructure? Is it being caused by external factors such as economic change, government change or changing business environments? Does it come from our own insecurities? In your organisation, taking the time to speak to your teams, and identifying and understanding where their fear is coming from, will assist them to let it go more quickly.

Be aware, though, that fear may actually be coming from you as a leader. Did you know that fear, panic and negative emotions are contagious? If you as a leader are not yet resistant to fear, or have yet to master it, that may be affecting your team also. Fear is an incredibly powerful emotion, one that is embedded and has evolved with us to help us to protect ourselves, to fight or flee, to survive.

So, what should we do after we identify the source of fear? We need to address our response to this fear and the often-associated state of panic. While we shouldn't completely push these emotions away (they are vital survival instincts after all) we also shouldn't let them take over our lives. We cannot be ruled by fear and panic. Instead of letting these emotions own us, we need to remember that we own them.

Here are a couple of ways you can do that:

1. Firstly, and most simply, fear and its contamination can be controlled by the simple practices of mindfulness and meditation, which can clear your mind and focus your energy on more positive ways. This can move you from a narrow focus, reacting to any stimulus as it comes along, to a more proactive, wider view. This allows for more options and possibilities. If your mind is clear, focused and not in a reactive trap, you can more easily see, think and utilise your invaluable sense of intuition.

2. Secondly, take time to define (or re-define) your values. Create a clear picture of what really matters to you, and what deeply drives you and impacts you, then you can open yourself up beyond the emotion of fear or panic and into deeper parts of yourself. We are more than our fear. We are bigger than that; fear is not what makes us. We are also made up of our intentions, our wisdom, our compassion, and our beliefs, and these are all honed through our senses. Mindfulness and the strengths of our values are delivered through clear minds. We cannot let our fear control us.

To help you reconnect with your true self amidst chaos, and rekindle a sense of who you are, here is a simple exercise. Sit down for a couple of minutes with pen and paper in front of you, then ask yourself this question: *Even in the midst of this chaos, who do I want to be?*

Although she did not have a piece of paper in the confines of her hiding place, Rukhsana (in the previous chapter) asked herself these questions: *What do I want to be? Do I want to be abducted and condemned to a life of dutiful slavery, mistreatment or possible death? Or do I want to take control of the situation, embrace the fear, do something more positive, and attempt to lead my family to safety?*

This simple exercise is an incredibly powerful protection against the spread of fear. Both Rukhsana and her brother were extremely fearful in hiding. But Rukhsana did not let this dictate her behaviour. Practising mindfulness, she made a decision, a conscious choice, to be a leader and build a plan of action to deliver on the decision. She could have easily remained hidden, risking being found and taken against her will. She would have been forgiven for not resisting. But she acted. In the moments before her heroic decision, Rukhsana clarified her values and her purpose in her mind. She then used the energy of fear to drive action and lead an assault on what threatened her and her family. She chose to be selfless. She chose to take control of an uncontrollable situation. To protect herself and those she loved.

These stories of courageous leadership are inspiring, but when it comes to our day-to-day lives, how do we become courageous and inspiring leaders? Below are six points that I believe are key:

- **Be available for the tough conversations:** Courageous leadership is about being uncomfortable. It's about being honest. Have those tough conversations, don't put them off. Situations often get worse with time if not addressed. Have the conversations early and have them with purpose and kindness.
- **Control fears and feelings:** As we saw in the story of Rukhsana, control of your feelings and fears enables you to lead with courage. Directing the energy that these provide into positive behaviour can deliver powerful results.
- **Use setbacks as steppingstones:** Courageous leaders use setbacks as learning opportunities. This is a growth mindset. Think about the magical WD-40 spray that is so popular for preventing rust and freeing up metal locks, hinges, etc. It's called WD-40, because it was the fortieth formula that the

makers tried, and the one that finally worked. The other thirty-nine could have been seen as setbacks and failures, but the team used them as steppingstones and learning opportunities to get to the final product.

- **Have an action bias:** Many leaders today are hesitant to act, perhaps through fear of repercussions, fear of making the wrong decision, or fear of making mistakes. But these are not courageous leaders. Courageous leaders have an action bias. Using a clear mind, delivered through the mastery of fear, they formulate a plan that will work and deliver it. In times of adversity, they are out there, leading from the front, delivering positive change and inspiring their teams to follow them.

- **Be inclusive and diverse:** Our workplaces are evolving to become more inclusive and diverse, utilising the wide and varied skill sets that are available because of different viewpoints, different cultures, different perspectives, and different approaches. Courageous leaders are not threatened by these differences; they embrace them to build and strengthen their teams. They enhance performance and results through using diversity, along with a growth mindset, to influence and deliver change. To deliver results.

- **Avoid shame and blame:** Courageous leaders don't play the blame game and shame their teams or those around them if something goes wrong. Courageous leaders are willing to be vulnerable, authentic and resilient. They value a growth mindset, and the opportunities for growth and improvement that are available when things don't go quite to plan. They take responsibility for the good and the not-so-good outcomes. They continue to learn. To encourage and inspire those around them.

It takes courageous leadership, backed up with a mindset that is open and willing to adapt and change, to be successful. It takes courage to turn up and forge forward, even if you don't know what the outcome will be. It takes courage to know that even when you can't predict the outcome, there is one thing that is for sure—there is a learning opportunity. Whether things go well or go badly, have the courage to embrace the outcomes and learn and grow from them.

'The courage to be vulnerable is not about winning or losing, it's about the courage to show up when you can't predict or control the outcome.'

BRENÉ BROWN, AUTHOR OF 'DARE TO LEAD'

Write down 5 insights and actions from this chapter to specifically help you face your own fears:

- ....

- ....

- ....

- ....

- ....

Courageous Thoughts

Courage is resistance to fear and mastery
of fear, not absence of fear.

To be a courageous leader, you don't necessarily need
a title or recognition; you just need to have mastered
your fear, be resistant to it, and have an action bias.

Create a clear picture of what really matters to you,
and what deeply drives you and impacts you, then
you can open yourself up beyond the emotion of
fear or panic and into deeper parts of yourself.

THE COURAGE COMPASS™

'It is only through labour and painful effort, by grim energy and resolute courage that we move on to better things.'

THEODORE ROOSEVELT

THE COMPASS

'In this world, you have a soul for a compass and a heart for a pair of wings.'

MARY CHAPIN CARPENTER, SINGER-SONGWRITER

I n the complexity of our hectic lives today, our vision of the world around us can become clouded—tangled, unclear and seemingly complicated by obstacles. A clear indication of our best pathway sometimes won't materialise, no matter how we try. The direction we should be going in can become obscured by blockers in our way.

I've had this experience myself. Somehow, sometimes we lose focus and find ourselves in a situation where we can't see the forest for the trees. We need to negotiate our way around the blockers and through the clouds. As people and as leaders, we need a reliable tool to guide us in these situations.

To handle times of crisis or adversity, we need courage. That in turn requires us to be clear about our own values, so we can be guided by our morality to act in the appropriate way. As a result, we become clear about our intentions and purpose, and therefore more selfless, more mindful, more agile, more focused and more connected.

What are the values and morals that guide our behaviours in these situations? That enable us to be courageous leaders and display courageous leadership? These are the points of our Courage Compass™.

WHAT IS A COURAGE COMPASS™?

I love this metaphor; it's one of my favourites. After spending 25 years in the leadership industry, with over a decade of research and work in the leadership space, the one thing I rely on and focus on is my Courage Compass™. It is the most powerful tool a leader can have and I'm excited to share it with you. So, let's start breaking it down.

I'm not sure if you have seen the 2002 movie 'My Big Fat Greek Wedding', but I'm going to borrow from one of the father's favourite conversation points in that movie ... the origin of a word. In the original Latin version, the word 'compass' is separated into two pieces: 'com' meaning 'together' and 'passus' meaning 'a step'. Using this definition, as leaders our compass allows us to guide the steps of our teams together and in a specific direction.

And what direction is that? It is the direction determined by our purpose, driven by courage and delivering courageous behaviours. Using our Courage Compass™, we guide our teams selflessly, building them up, providing them with the tools they need, and enabling them to achieve success. We lead through example, using the following four points on the Courage Compass™:

KINDNESS IMPACT PURPOSE RESILIENCE

Why a compass? It shows the direction we need to head in order to achieve our goal. Regardless of the type of obstacle in our path, we can use a compass to circumnavigate it and get back on track quickly and easily.

How many times in our lives or in our leadership roles do we take a step back and reflect on our direction or path? In turn, how many times do we, as leaders or within our teams, want to be courageous and yet let fear get in the way?

A compass can be our most powerful tool when we are seeking the right direction. A Courage Compass™ is there for us when we need guidance as we navigate through change, and we need confidence in our chosen path or action—a Courage Compass™ underpinned by mindset, intention and habits.

Before GPS navigation systems and high-tech mapping, sailors used compasses to guide their ships safely through treacherous waters. They set their target destination on their map and relied on their compass to help them maintain the right trajectory. It was perhaps the most important piece of equipment on the ship, as it showed whether the ship was on or off course. It also allowed them to guide the ship around a dangerous obstacle or avoid a hazard in their way, then easily get back on their right course.

In a leadership situation, your Courage Compass™ helps you to circumnavigate dangers and obstacles and return your 'ship' to its original course, continuously moving towards your ultimate destination, regardless of what has been in your way.

As you already know, I love the Japanese culture, its complexity and its intricacies. I love that it is very distinctive. That it is marvellously multi-faceted. However, the Japanese culture is also rapidly evolving. Advancements in technology, the adoption of a democratic system of government, and a population boom have meant the culture has had to adapt to these changes and also to evolving lifestyles. These changes can also mean the loss of traditional values and beliefs that are incredibly influential culturally. But, in the face of these challenges, the Japanese culture has adapted very well, maintaining a delicate balance between the traditional and the modern. Their traditional roots remain strong. Values of respect, politeness, courtesy and graciousness still underpin society.

How is this possible? It is because certain foundational concepts remain at the core of their behaviours, attitudes and cultural directions—belonging, harmony, group orientation, politeness, modesty, gentleness, patience and formality.

While the Japanese culture's version of a compass seems to have a large number of points on the rose, that does not impact its effectiveness. These concepts guide Japanese society through change, clearly reinforcing what matters as things evolve. This compass provides constant destination points and anchor points that all journeys must align with.

As leaders today, we face similar change and hazards in life, in business and in leadership. Some dangers are obvious, some are hidden, but all require a compass to navigate around or through safely.

As in Japanese culture and society, if we as leaders have a definite direction, a clear destination and strong values as compass points to guide us along the way, we will adapt and evolve efficiently and effectively. We will face challenges and conquer them, not only maintaining our values and morals, but using them to drive us and achieve success.

Using our compass, we can make decisions with certainty. With courage. We can act with kindness. We can act with purpose. We can act with resilience. We have impact.

HOW DO YOU BUILD YOUR COURAGE COMPASS™?

How do you strengthen your compass's power and impact? There are a small variety of tools available in the market today that can help you (not as many as there should be!) and I also recommend the following: to develop your own compass and let it drive courageous leadership, you can take our **Courage Compass™ Leadership Self or 360 Assessments**. (See the 'Reference' section at the end of this book to find the link to our website.)

These tools will help show your existing strengths, points for improvement, and points of growth. They will help embed the compass values in your psyche, in your subconscious, so you have them as an innate behaviour model to drive instinctive responses. This will help give you strength and clarity to lead with courage.

When I need to tap into my courage, I always look to my compass. In the following chapters, we expand on the points of the Courage Compass™ and look at how you can use them to be a courageous leader today, in all aspects of your life.

Write down 5 insights and actions from this chapter about your own Courage Compass™:

- ....

- ....

- ....

- ....

- ....

Courageous Thoughts

Our Courage Compass™ guides our behaviour as leaders, helping to guide our teams selflessly, build them up and enable them to achieve success.

Using our compass, we can make decisions with certainty. With courage. We can act with kindness. We can act with purpose. We can act with resilience. We have impact. We drive positive cultures.

COURAGE IS KINDNESS

'Too often we underestimate the power of a touch, a smile, a kind word, a listening ear, an honest compliment, or the smallest act of caring, all of which have the potential to turn a life around.'

LEO BUSCAGLIA (DR. LOVE), AUTHOR & SPEAKER

D oes kindness in leadership really matter? Let's take a moment to reflect. At the end of your career, what would you like people to say when they think back on you as a leader? At the culmination of a very successful career, what would you like your defining accomplishment to be? What if your crowning achievement was your kindness as a leader?

Kindness is the first and most prominent point on our Courage Compass™, the north point. Let's reflect on an example to illustrate.

> Someone once asked Princess Diana how she would like to be remembered if she became queen. Her response? *'I'd like to be a queen of people's hearts.'*

> If that were her only life mission, that alone would have been her resounding success. She became known as the people's princess and is remembered for her kindness. She developed a reputation for working tirelessly for charities and causes that were close to her heart. Princess Diana recognised that she was in a unique position to help others and to use her fame to become a leader in kindness. She did not have an easy life, although it looked glamourous. She had personal demons to fight and conquer. However, these challenges gave her the empathy to lead with courage and kindness. She grew to lead with fearlessness and with compassion.

What is kindness? It's officially defined as the qualities of friendliness, generosity and consideration. As leaders this means being friendly to your teams, being generous with your time and praise, and being considerate of their individual needs and feelings. Understanding their goals, dreams and motivations. Helping individuals to achieve their own vision of their future.

Where does kindness begin? It begins within. Susan David, psychologist on the faculty of Harvard Medical School, explains that '*People who have greater levels of self-compassion tend to be more motivated, less lazy, and more successful over time. But just as important, they like themselves, even when they fall short*'.

It is only when we can show kindness to ourselves and accept that discomfort, stress, pain and sadness are all a part of life, that we can accept that in others and show kindness to them.

Kindness is a leadership behaviour that inspires those around you to accept the vision you see for the group. They then follow you out of mutual respect, consideration and genuine pleasure from being around you and being aligned with your vision and goals.

Kindness in leadership is being considerate—considerate of other people's positions, their viewpoints, drivers, motivators, feelings—and learning from diversity of thought and perspective.

It is these attributes of kindness that we see and admire in Princess Diana's story, exemplified, for example, by her friendliness towards those suffering from HIV and leprosy, holding their hands and showing she cared.

> Princess Diana was generous with her time for the causes she supported. She took time out of her schedule to go out of her way to hug children who had been disadvantaged. She was generous with her time in advocating for the removal of landmines and supporting those whose lives had been, or potentially might be, affected by them.

She was considerate of other people's feelings and positions in life, using her position, fame and power to advocate for them, to help them get the support they needed to live better lives. Most of all she was a leader. Her charisma, manner and kindness meant that people were naturally drawn towards her and attracted to her goals, and also wanted to make a positive change in the world they lived in.

But kindness in leadership hasn't always had (and you could argue, still doesn't have) the focus that it deserves in leadership theory and thinking. It is my experience that kindness is not always considered part of strong leadership. It is not encouraged. Not taught.

Isn't this something that we should be teaching, though? A lot of the strong leaders in history that we as a society have a great affection for—like Princess Diana and Mother Teresa—were driven by kindness. Isn't this something that should be taught with all leaders? In all situations?

In the words of the Dalai Lama XIV: '*Love and compassion are necessities, not luxuries. Without them, humanity cannot survive.*' I argue that this applies more importantly in leadership. Kindness, shown through compassion and consideration of another person's situation, is a leadership essential. It is the most prominent point on the Courage Compass™—the north point that all other points align to, and which should be the strongest leadership driver.

In the context of leadership, kindness empowers people to lead with positivity, purpose and open-mindedness. It empowers leaders to embrace new ideas and encourages trust. If leaders show kindness, they accelerate trust, and in turn create happier, more empowered employees, who will be inspired to deliver better results.

Let's just explore those 'better results' for a moment. Does kindness really pay off in terms of business performance? Can you be kind as a leader, and still be effective in our profit-driven, cut-throat world? I know some leaders who are striving to lead with courage and with kindness. They are doing this while also managing to build their profit line. They are placing their people first, but also delivering against their objectives and targets, keeping their stakeholders happy year on year. It is possible. It is essential. There is a plethora of research around this, and the data supports the outcome that kindness always delivers.

Research by Berkley University shows there are definitely improved financial and performance results for those businesses that include kindness as a fundamental in the way they do things, and in their values. Their 2013 survey shows that healthcare claims for employees with high levels of stress were 46 percent higher than in organisations with lower levels of stress. It also showed that 52 percent of employees reported that workplace stress led them to look for a new job, leave a job, or refuse additional responsibilities or promotions.

Berkley University researchers say the solution is compassion. What Berkley means by compassion is what we have called kindness here. Compassion or kindness in leadership has proven to deliver happier workplaces, reduce healthcare costs for employees, reduce absenteeism and also reduce turnover. Not only this, kindness or compassion also improves the bottom-line.

A 2015 global study done collaboratively by McKinsey, Stanford, and the London School of Economics showed that a one-point improvement in a company's management practices (adding in kindness and compassion) is worth as much as a 25 percent increase in your labour force, or a 65 percent increase in the amount of invested capital. It's not just a warm fuzzy ideal. Building kindness into your leadership style, business and culture truly can affect your bottom-line. Greatly.

In the words of Maya Angelou: *'People will forget what you said. People will forget what you did. But people will never forget how you made them feel.'*

Today we live in a survival-of-the-fittest world. A world where we live at a hectic pace. We can all relate to this, can't we? We never have enough time, and as leaders, we are often most guilty of being time poor, of being completely driven by and focused on results. In this environment it's very easy for kindness to take second place, or even last place behind the demands of the pressures we are faced with. I've been guilty of it myself, of losing a level of kindness in the rush to get things done quickly, of being short with people when it was not necessary. (But then, is it ever necessary?)

In this fast-paced business world, technology has offered endless opportunities for efficiency, and we have become slaves to it. We trade in knowledge, proficiency, competency and efficiency. We have taken the impact of human connection out of the equation. Human interaction is becoming a casualty of efficiency, with artificial intelligence and automation being adopted to drive cost savings, to make more profit. And it has changed the way we interact, the way we lead. Kindness and compassion have taken a back seat, and that is, ironically, ultimately affecting our bottom-line, the wellbeing of our staff and our performance.

What sets us humans apart from machines is our ability to act with empathy, to feel, to be intuitive, to be compassionate and to act with kindness. In leadership, considering the human toll and impact of the decisions we make is what gives us the edge over artificial intelligence.

These skills allow us to lead our teams with kindness, with strength and with spirit. This type of leadership takes courage.

HOW DO WE TAKE ACTION AND LEAD WITH KINDNESS?

Global research shows, and my experience backs this up, that if you focus on the following you will be well on your way to being a kind and compassionate leader:

- **Truly appreciate your team:** This means genuinely and sincerely celebrating their successes by showing that you legitimately care and are concerned about your team member's individual wellbeing, their development, their achievements.
- **Give your team the freedom to be inspired and source inspiration:** This is the freedom to expand their network, gaining inspiration from as wide a range of colleagues and as wide a group of people as possible. Encourage them to build meaningful connections, encouraging all connections to be underpinned by respect and kindness.
- **Encourage your teams to appreciate and respect people with differing opinions:** Kindness in teams is being open to new perspectives of others in order to enrich your own perspective. Kindness in leadership is encouraging diversity of thought, rich dialogue and respectful differences.
- **Kind leadership is having tough conversations:** You must be prepared to let your team know when they are not meeting expectations and give them guidance on points of improvement. Doing this with sincerity, authenticity and compassion will build stronger relationships and inspire them, in turn, to have their own honest, constructive conversations, building collaboration and trust across organisations.

So, what do kind leaders do on a day-to-day basis?

- **Kind leaders bring authenticity.** They are transparent in their dealings, and they act with warmth, building trust and empowering their followers to achieve beyond any self-imposed boundaries. Kind leaders have the courage to have difficult conversations if it is in the best interest of their team member's growth and development. But they are handled with genuine care that comes from wanting the best for the person involved.
- **Kind leaders encourage individuals in their teams** to be the best versions of themselves, to shine, to be courageous, without selfish intentions. Kind leaders accept that there may be members of their teams who may surpass even their own skills, and that's okay. Having the kindness and courage to accept this without limiting another's potential is a most powerful leadership style and approach.
- **Kind leaders be kind to themselves.** Remember the oxygen mask and take that first before assisting others.

The psychology behind the impact of kindness is that emotions are contagious—actually, more contagious than the world's worst pandemic. Just think for a minute: if someone cuts you off in traffic in the morning, it can really put a shadow over the rest of your day, and you can pass this on to others in your team when you are short with them. Unhappy teams are less productive due to the emotional debt that they are working through at that point in time.

On the flipside, if you land a rock-star car park, the lift is waiting, and someone compliments your outfit on your way into work in the morning, you will be walking on cloud nine! You are far more likely to have a much better day and pass this sunshiny attitude onto your team.

I know we have mentioned some research already, but I can't resist adding a couple of more statistics to support my point. Warwick University, in the United Kingdom, carried out a study that showed that businesses with happy staff are 12 percent more productive than their counterparts with unhappy staff. Google found in 2018 that when they invested in employee support services, their staff satisfaction rating rose by 37 percent, leading to higher productivity. The conclusion supports what I have been saying for years—acting with kindness in business really pays off and it does impact the bottom line.

Intentional leadership based on strong understanding, good motives, and a desire to do the best for those around us, is needed in our world today. In our businesses today. It's simple. Emotions drive us, and emotions are contagious. So, if you want a productive and happy workforce, you must create it.

But, if kindness is so simple, possible and essential to a successful business, why do we as today's leaders find it so challenging?

For one, kindness is often associated with being weak, and this is not the look any leader wants. But being a kind leader doesn't mean being a weak leader. Great leaders can be very capable of making strong business decisions and having tough conversations. They just do it with kindness. Here's an example to illustrate the point:

Mary Barra has been the chairman and CEO of General Motors Company since 2014. She is the first female head of an auto manufacturer and is widely regarded as one of the most powerful women in the world.

She is known for her quiet, humble and kind leadership style, but she is a courageous leader. During her first year as CEO with the company, Mary issued 84 safety recalls for over 30 million cars world-wide, placing the safety of vehicle owners above company profits. She was summonsed to testify in a Senate hearing regarding the vehicle recalls and deaths that had allegedly been caused by a faulty ignition switch in some vehicles. She had tough conversations. She stood up for those who could not stand up for themselves. She drove the creation of new policies that encouraged workers to report problems that they came across in the business, giving people a voice and a channel to be heard, which in turn changed company culture.

In view of this example, I'm throwing down the challenge to you now. Will you join me in being a leader that shows both strength and kindness? There's nothing weak about that.

So, I can hear you asking … *How do I become a strong, kind leader? What steps do I need to take?*

Here are five points that will help you on your way:

- **Set clear expectations:** Provide a clear sense of direction and definite goals. Set out clearly in writing exactly what you see the team's role as; the individual's role and contribution to that; how you expect people to act; what you expect them to achieve; and how you expect to interact with them and support them. Be clear. Be concise.

- **Give genuine, honest feedback and encourage growth:** Tell the truth. Avoiding telling the whole truth so that you don't hurt someone's feelings is not being kind. This approach deprives the person of an opportunity to grow. Your role as a leader is to mentor your teams, to help them achieve their best. It's all about self-actualisation at this point, helping to create opportunities to fulfil your team member's personal goals, to reach their potential. Leaders need to tell the truth in an authentic, genuine, sincere and kind way. With the intention of supporting growth and development, genuine feedback and encouraging growth in your team will place them en route to becoming fulfilled, satisfied and high performing. In my world I model this behaviour with my beautiful daughter. My goal is to help lead her through her formative years by providing honest feedback, gently guiding her in the right direction and encouraging her growth.

- **Be transparent in your decisions:** Showing consideration and openness in your decision-making demonstrates kindness. It doesn't matter whether the impact on an individual member of your team is large or small, positive or negative. It is your role as a leader to provide your team with the back-story, adding some dimension and understanding to how you came to your decision. Whether your team agrees or not, understanding where you are coming from can help your team get on board. Showing your approach to decisions will give people certainty and confidence in you in the future, reducing stress and other negative cultural impacts that are often associated with change. It's a strong and positive approach. It takes courage. It takes resilience. It delivers results.

- **Treat people like people, not numbers:** This is the absolute foundation of kindness in leadership. It can be far too easy to treat people as numbers, especially if you are making difficult decisions around downsizing or restructuring teams. But realising people are people, and treating them that way, with respect, will show that you are genuinely here for the right reasons. Show them that they are important to you and the business. How do you do this? You acknowledge them, celebrate successes, check in to see if they are okay. Respect them and they will, in turn, respect you.

- **Decide where you can create an impact on a broader scale:** This could be in your local community, your country or globally—you could lead a movement that will serve future generations.

Using these steps, kind leaders will facilitate a happier, more profitable workforce.

HOW DOES KINDNESS PLAY OUT IN YOUR DAILY WORLD?

It takes courage to be kind. Extending kindness and compassion to others, and even to ourselves, risks judgment, rejection and being seen as going against the norm in some organisational cultures. Sometimes it means we make ourselves vulnerable, which might be uncomfortable, but in the long run it leaves us in a position of strength.

Are you seeing kindness as a weakness when it is actually a strength? I challenge you to build your leadership capabilities with this super-power. Use your courage to build kindness and compassion into your practices, relationships and interactions and you will definitely see the benefits.

Remember to be kind to yourself too.

'A kind life is fundamentally
a life of courage.'

WAYNE MULLER, AUTHOR, MENTOR, THERAPIST, MINISTER

———————————————————

Write down 5 insights and actions from this chapter that show how you would like kindness to play out in your world:

- ....

- ....

- ....

- ....

- ....

Courageous Thoughts

Kindness in leadership is being generous with your time. It is making time for your team, understanding their goals, dreams and motivations, and helping them to achieve their individual vision of their future. It is being considerate of other people's positions, their viewpoints, their drivers, their motivators, their feelings.

Kindness empowers people to lead with positivity, purpose, and open-mindedness. It empowers leaders to embrace new ideas.

If leaders show kindness, they accelerate trust and in turn create happier, more empowered employees, who will be inspired to deliver better results, be more productive and deliver a more profitable bottom-line for the business.

COURAGE IS IMPACT

'Genius is in the idea. Impact, however, comes from action.'

SIMON SINEK, AUTHOR OF 'START WITH WHY'

Have you had experience in leading with impact or worked with a leader who had impact? What does 'impact' mean to you?

Impact is the second point on our Courage Compass™. According to Lexico (an Oxford dictionary website), impact is defined as a marked effect or influence one person has on another through contact. While these situations of impact can occur at any point and in any circumstance, the greatest consequence is often felt in difficult or adverse times.

I am sure this definition triggers memories of people who have impacted you in your life so far. Let's expand this definition and explore how impact results from courageous and kind leadership.

Impact means change, either positive or negative, and can manifest in many different aspects of our lives, such as health, status, wealth, knowledge, skill, behaviour, and more. Impact can definitely have a long-term effect, either directly or indirectly, and can be either intended or unintended. When handled with a growth mindset, impact, in these terms, often results in development for everyone involved.

In leadership, it's important that your impact be direct and intentional for it to be most powerful. It is equally important that in the context of the impact you are aiming to have on your team, your business or the people around, you are positive, developing the best cause-and-effect relationships with intention.

Courageous, impactful leadership is motivating and inspiring to those around you. It helps them to set higher personal and professional goals, and then achieve them. Your leadership, delivered with kindness and impact, can stimulate a desire for personal growth in your team members, and encourage its achievement. Use kindness and understanding to lead your teams, to inspire the individuals within them to join you on a journey of discovery and progression.

It's also incredibly important when leading with courage and impact, to also lead with authenticity, with genuine legitimacy and not just an intermittent approach. Walk the walk and talk the talk; lead by example and inspire others through your own actions and integrity. An isolated incident, action or situation will not deliver this result. It takes a genuine, consistent, long-term approach and ongoing commitment to positive change to deliver sustainable and self-reinforcing results.

Who has had this level of impact in your life? This question got me thinking about my life also. To be honest, there have been a lot of people who have impacted me my journey. They are scattered across my life like gems, shining at times when they were most needed; there to provide guidance, comfort and some much-wanted direction. One person who stands out in my memory is a teacher in primary school.

During my early school years, I suffered crippling anxiety and an almost tangible fear of failing. In reality, I was a high-achieving student, and I was also one of, if not the hardest working students around. But it was my lack of confidence that led to and drove my anxiety and fear. It was debilitating. It was holding me back from achieving my potential.

At that point in my life, I thought that being the best and smartest would help me overcome my anxiety and fear. My thought process was that if you know you are the best, why would you be anxious about failing? Isn't that, right? You would just always be the best!

But this caused a vicious cycle of pressure on myself, of feeling like I had no other option than to maintain the ultimate level of achievement; to maintain what felt like a facade. This behaviour, in fact, fed my anxiety and my crippling fear of failing.

My year-seven teacher recognised my behaviours and this cycle. He recognised and completely believed in my potential. He recognised my lack of self-confidence and self-limiting behaviours. He knew the only thing that was holding me back from achieving my potential was me and my fears.

He not only recognised my needs, but he also took an interest in me. Through his belief in me and his guidance, he gave me the courage to be myself. This was not an unsustainable version of myself, it was just me. My true self.

He helped me understand that I didn't need to put pressure on myself to always be the best, to always be at the top of the class. All I needed was to be the greatest I could be. For me. I did not need to be perfect, I just needed to believe in myself, to build my self-confidence and truly believe that I could do whatever I really committed myself to. Even if I made a mistake, if I was not achieving the ultimate at the moment, it was ok. He helped me to see that life was a journey of growth and development. And it happens over time.

This teacher had a profound impact on me, and he inspired me to just be me. To embrace who I was. To be real. To be honest. To be kind to myself. To continue to grow but not put pressure on myself. He encouraged me to see that the journey was what mattered, and that you needed to go on the journey to achieve sustainable change. He taught me to have courage. He taught me with kindness. For a troubled teenager, his was leadership with impact. And it made a significant change in my life.

This was not just talk, though. My teacher gave me strategies and an action plan to move forward. He gave me tools to use. Behaviours to model. He encouraged me to act with confidence and trust that in time true confidence would follow; to take opportunities to build my belief in myself.

It's what true courageous leaders do. Just speaking about having an impact and making a difference is not enough. There must be action. Leaders with impact have an action bias. For example, reflect on the life of Aung San Suu Kyi.

> An action bias drove Aung San Suu Kyi in the early years of her political career. Suu Kyi was a politician who fought valiantly against military rule and for democracy in the country of Myanmar. She fought for human rights and freedom of the press. She received a Nobel Peace Prize in recognition of her work and for the positive impact it had on the country she loved. She endured nearly two decades of house arrest for her views and actions. Throughout this whole time, she led with impact. She delivered positive change in the lives of the people she loved, and the country she fought for. It's an amazing example of the true power of courageous, impactful leaders.

However, Aung San Suu Kyi also showed what happens when leading with impact goes wrong. When it is misguided. When the outcome of leading with impact is negative. Her story is, unfortunately, a masterclass in how to influence for destruction.

When finally released from house arrest, and after being elected to political power in the country, Aung San Suu Kyi's talk continued, however her action stopped. She lost her power of positive action for good. She lost her action bias. She became caught in the trap of using her position and leadership to support negative outcomes for the people she once fought for.

She failed to champion and influence change when she was in power. In this situation, the end of action ultimately led to a change in attitude and perspective. There is also a basic human behaviour in effect here—cognitive dissonance. This is the discomfort when your beliefs and behaviours are not aligned. In order to align these again, your beliefs are far easier to change than your behaviours. Even someone in Suu Kyi's position was not immune to the impacts of a cognitive dissonance state.

This loss of an action bias also led to a change in behaviour in Suu Kyi. It's a trap that leaders must be aware of and continue to consciously avoid. Her values, beliefs and behaviours were no longer aligned, and her persona and leadership approach changed to suit. She became authoritarian, supporting the military and the forces that she once fought. Allegations have also been made that she excused genocide and ethnic cleansing. This led to the loss of her Nobel Prize, but more tragically for Suu Kyi, it meant the loss of her beliefs, her authenticity.

Without the right context and the right drivers, supported by an action bias, leading with impact can return negative results. This leads to a situation that is not conducive to better people, a better society, better communities or a better world. It becomes destructive and harmful. It causes negative impacts and outcomes and will ultimately fail.

So, what enables a leader to avoid this negative trap and instead lead with courage and kindness to deliver positive impact? It's not about wearing the latest and most expensive branded clothing. It's not about the car you drive. It's not about the people you are connected with. Or how you use your connections. Leading with courage and impact is about:

- **An attitude of service:** Conducting yourself with an intention to serve your team, your community, your organisation. Being a servant leader. This will allow you to genuinely connect with people, earning their trust and influencing them in positive ways. This drives authenticity and genuineness.

- **Leading with purpose:** You can't lead blindly. It's physically impossible. As a leader with impact, you must lead with foresight—with purpose and direction for both yourself and for the team. It's about leading through example, setting a goal that is relatable and achievable, and working towards it. Using this direction to inspire and motivate your teams. Celebrating victories, successes and achievements along the way.

- **Being generous with your time and energy and participating in your team:** This sounds very much like kindness! And yes, they are linked. People need to feel supported and be supported through this experience, and kindness is the best way to do this. Generosity of time and energy from leadership creates a sense of belonging and of personal importance in team members. If your team members feel they and their contributions are valued and important to achieving the common goals, they will be more motivated, involved and more resilient to the hiccups that inevitably happen along the way.

- **Leading by example:** It's been said many times, and it can't be overstated—leading through example by modelling positive behaviours, continuously learning, having a growth mindset, learning from your failures and working with resilience to overcome obstacles is the strongest tool in your leading-with-impact toolbox. It's been proven time and again to deliver high performing results. It is critical, there are no two ways about it.

- **Fostering a culture of inclusiveness:** Inclusiveness and diversity of thoughts, beliefs and viewpoints are your keys to success. As a leader, ignoring biases as you build your teams will deliver the best results. Promote talent, regardless of how it is packaged. Acknowledge diversity and different perspectives. Encourage healthy debate and constructive challenging.

- **Managing conflict and negativity effectively:** As a leader, it's your duty to have those tough conversations, to call out negative behaviours and challenge them to be changed into positive actions. In an earlier chapter, we mentioned the example of the young leader and his epiphany of the power of having courageous, tough conversations. That story also supports the important point that to be effective, you must conduct these difficult conversations with kindness. This provides a safe working environment for people to perform at their optimum.

- **Building collaboration:** Being part of a tribe is a basic and essential human trait. And it's at risk of being lost in our individualistic world today. Building collaboration in your team underpins the development of diversity. It builds strength across teams and supports achievement. It enables access to diverse skills and different viewpoints to enrich outcomes and ensure they are sustainable.

In leading with impact, emotional intelligence is critical. Being very aware of the direct and indirect results of your leadership actions, and the impacts these have on those around you, is incredibly important. If you identify and contemplate your actions, you have the opportunity to amplify the positive and reduce the negative impacts that you have on those around you.

Awareness of the intentional and unintentional impacts of your leadership is critical. We all need to be on guard to ensure that even our smallest unintentional actions do not negatively impinge on those around us and their own journeys. Regardless of whether an action was intentional or not, the result or impact on others is mostly the same. So be aware of this and make sure you only deliver positive influences.

This is definitely tough. It means that as leaders we need to be constantly checking in and maintaining our situational awareness. But it's necessary to be successful. Being a leader with impact can change the world. Creating positive impressions on those around you will inspire changes in behaviours and beliefs. Being a courageous and kind leader will drive positive change and allow you to lead with impact.

'The only limit to your impact is your imagination and commitment.'

TONY ROBBINS, SPEAKER AND COACH

Write down 5 insights and actions from this chapter that will help you take action and create impact:

- ....

- ....

- ....

- ....

- ....

Courageous Thoughts

Impact means change to people's lives. It can be change that is positive or negative, but always has long-term effects.

Leading with impact can be through direct or indirect actions and intentional or unintentional activities. Be aware of these.

Leading with positive impact requires the application of courageous leadership traits, a strong purpose, and a high level of kindness.

COURAGE IS PURPOSE

*'Nothing is more creative
... nor destructive ...
than a brilliant mind
with a purpose.'*

DAN BROWN, AUTHOR

A daughter and her father were having a heart-to-heart conversation one day. The daughter was confiding that she was having a hard time finding a clear purpose to follow in life. She was also struggling to see why this was even important at all. This is how the story goes.

The girl's father was a chef, and in the way we all tend to, he resorted to something he knew well to help his daughter understand. He took her to the kitchen. There he filled three pots with water and placed each on the stove over a high heat. It only took a few minutes and the water in the three pots began to boil. In one boiling pot he placed potatoes. In the second boiling water pot he placed eggs. In the third boiling pot he placed ground coffee beans.

The father set a timer for 20 minutes and then sat in silence watching them. The daughter groaned and muttered, waiting impatiently and wondering what he was getting at. After 20 minutes, the timer chimed, so the father took the potatoes out of the water and placed them in a bowl. He took out the eggs and placed them in a second bowl. Finally, he poured the coffee into a mug.

'What do you see here?' he asked his daughter.

The daughter replied, 'Boiled potatoes, boiled eggs and coffee,' with more than a hint of sarcasm.

'Then you need to look closer,' the father said. 'Touch the potatoes. Feel the eggs. Taste the coffee.'

The daughter touched the potatoes and noticed they were soft. Her father then asked her to take an egg and break it. After peeling off the shell, she found the hard-boiled egg was bouncy and difficult to break. Finally, she took a sip of the coffee as he had asked. Its rich aroma brought a smile to her face and a little bit of sunshine to her morning. Who doesn't love a good coffee?

Then the father explained his point. It was all a matter of purpose and adversity. The potatoes, the eggs and coffee beans had each faced the same adversity—the boiling water—but each had a different purpose and because of this, each had reacted differently.

The potato went into the water hard, unrelenting and inedible. But in boiling water, quickly became soft and pliable, enjoyable to eat and also easily able to be transformed into a delicious mash, the best ever comfort food. The potato's ultimate purpose is to be a tasty, soft, comforting food. They nourish. They make you feel warm and satisfied.

The eggs, on the other hand, were fragile going into the water, with only a thin outer shell protecting their liquid centre. But under adversity, the inside of the egg became hard, it became resilient. It also became more easily edible and much more enjoyable as a snack. Their purpose is to be a nutritious, healthy, snack-sized and low-fuss meal.

The ground coffee beans were a different story altogether ... and by far the most unique. The coffee beans faced multiple adversities. They were roasted, ground and boiled. The first two adversities, the roast and grind, changed them. But after they were exposed to the boiling water, the third adversity, they changed it instead. They changed their surrounding environment to create something new, something wonderful, something that transforms the lives of those that drink it. The coffee beans' purpose is to provide energy. To uplift. To change the world through their influence.

Each reacted in a different way because of their purpose. Finding your purpose is important. As a leader, adversity may mean you need to be soft and comforting like the potato. You might need to be strong and provide nourishment like the egg. Or you may need to transform the environment and those around you like the coffee, to provide the energy and fire everyone up, inspiring them to action. It all depends on your purpose.

Purpose is the third point of our Courage Compass™. But what is purpose? In my research and in my experience, I've found purpose to be the reason why something is done, why something is created or why it exists. From a leadership perspective, it's the sense of resolve, of determination, that drives someone. It's a person's intention or objective and the expression of it.

Leaders need the following strategies to successfully integrate purpose:

- A clear vision, a direction to strive for, a goal or objective to hold your focus and keep you heading in the right direction
- A stable foundation to be grounded or anchored in and to build on, and to support you in the pursuit of your goal
- An intentional focus to keep energies and activities aligned, so things don't just happen randomly or on their own. Actions need to be intentional and carefully guided.
- Meaningful relationships to be part of the legacy being built, and to show you opportunities for improvement, as well as be catalysts for your vision and the drive for change

- Resilience to overcome obstacles that will definitely pop up in your pathway. It's the strength, persistence and tenacity in a courageous leader that really delivers results.
- A willingness to change, to adapt through a growth mindset, constantly looking for opportunities to improve and to do things better
- Sustainability through a long-lasting outcome, a legacy, with change that delivers value into the future, often long after our influence has faded.

We all know, though, that purpose can be misdirected. In the words of Dan Brown, who opened this chapter with his brilliant quote, nothing can be more creative or destructive than a strong purpose. It's a very scary thought, but Adolf Hitler had an incredibly strong purpose, and executed it with equal passion and vigour. It is widely agreed that he was a notable and strong leader, who led with passion and with purpose, and delivered with impact. Unfortunately, though, a majority of the world today agrees that this purpose was as misguided as it could be, and the impact of it was incredibly destructive.

I'm thankful, though, that there are many more positive than negative examples of great leadership impacting others. Every year we get a glimpse of people with purpose who have become leaders with purpose in their fields during the Order of Australia awards and similar award programs that are held locally, state-wide, nationally and internationally, such as the Nobel Prize and Global Achievement Awards. One example is outlined here for Professor Larissa Behrendt.

Professor Larissa Behrendt received an Order of Australia in 2020 for outstanding service to Indigenous education and research. Her achievements in the field of Law—becoming the first Indigenous woman to graduate from Harvard University and the youngest

114

female law professor in Australia, among other achievements—were noted with our highest honour. Larissa is a truly inspirational leader whose purpose to overcome disadvantage and show others they can achieve anything if they have a strong purpose will impact for years to come. She is likely to inspire an entire generation of up-and-coming young Australian women.

So, what makes a purpose-driven leader? It's not a specific set of characteristics that makes a leader with purpose, it is the alignment of values with a clear definition of success. Using the tools mentioned above, leaders with purpose provide a sense of meaning and wellbeing to their teams, inspiring and guiding them to attain goals.

What can you do to be a purpose-driven leader? The following have been proven to drive impactful purpose:

- Use meaningful, purpose-driven language that is both inspirational and action biased.
- Lead by example. A leader who knows their purpose and is personally driven by that purpose will inspire teams to follow.
- Focus on the strengths in yourself and your team, developing these, developing careers, inspiring and driving yourself and others to achieve aspirations.
- Develop inspiring statements of purpose for both your leadership and your goals, showing how you will lead.
- Work with your teams to also build statements of purpose for their own pathway, providing them with a strong foundation for improvement and a clear, defined direction and goal.
- Develop long-term and short-term goals for your leadership and your team as a collective, and for the individual members of your team. Find the quick wins that will build momentum and motivation to continue on the journey.

- Focus on future goals and work backwards to build a clear pathway to achieving them.
- As a leader with purpose, you need to be approachable, honest, encouraging, action biased, willing to have tough conversations, and real and authentic with your team.
- Maintain a holistic view for yourself and your team. Work matters, but life, family and wellbeing also matter. Keeping a balanced view of these will maintain resilience in your teams to help them achieve goals.

It's all a question of balance. An example I love is the ancient Chinese concept of Yin and Yang, which forms the basis of the ancient belief of Taoism.

Yin is the dark side of our experience. It is associated with everything that is hard, negative, cold and wet. Ironically, and in contrast to western belief, Yin is feminine. In contrast to Yin, Yang is the light side, associated with everything that is soft, warm, positive and dry. It is masculine in gender in the Chinese concept.

In Taoist belief, it is important that Yin and Yang are not seen as opposites, but that each side has a little bit of the other in it for balance. Yin can transform into Yang (cold into warm, hard into soft, you get the idea) and vice versa. In our example above, the potato, the egg and the coffee beans both turned from Yin into Yang, in accordance with their purpose.

In the context of leading with purpose, the best leadership styles are balanced, they are hard or resilient when needed, and they are soft and flexible when the situation calls for it. In Chinese mythology, it is said that the best things in life are at the confluence of the two forces. Its where there is a balance of both Yin and Yang that the best results are realised.

As leaders, this confluence is guiding with purpose, with impact, with kindness and with resilience, acknowledging the difficulties and obstacles and working to eliminate them. It is turning something hard (or an obstacle) into something that is fluid and easily removed from blocking your pathway. It is having difficult conversations for the benefit of development and turning these negative situations into positive growth. They are the attributes and behaviours of courageous leadership.

Satya Nadella, CEO of Microsoft, says of the 100,000+ people within Microsoft, 'I need to make sure we have a sense of purpose. It's about harmonizing multiple constituents, not just investors, customers, employees, partners. It's about all of them.'

The CEO of Otis Elevators, Judy Marks, summarises leading with purpose well. She stated that: '*Leadership with purpose is setting the vision and sharing it. Creating an environment where people can resonate not only with the mission, but also with its delivery.*'

Judy saw that her main role as a leader was to create an environment that allowed her team to achieve; an environment that was positive, inspiring, and purpose-driven and empowered. She worked with her team to eliminate obstacles in the pathway and to help guide the team to ultimately reach their goals.

Write down 5 insights and actions from this chapter that will help you to ensure you are a purpose-driven leader:

- ....

- ....

- ....

- ....

- ....

Courageous Thoughts

Leaders with purpose inspire their teams to work
together to achieve a shared goal through gaining
the trust and respect of team members.

Your role as a leader is to create an environment that
allows your team to achieve; an environment that is
positive, inspiring, purpose-driven and empowering.

COURAGE IS RESILIENCE

'Life is filled with unanswered questions, but it is the courage to seek those answers that continues to give meaning to life. You can spend your life wallowing in despair, wondering why you were the one who was led towards the road strewn with pain, or you can be grateful that you are strong enough to survive it.'

J.D. STROUBE, AUTHOR

B eing strong enough to survive life's obstacles, difficulties and unanswered questions is what we know as resilience. Resilience allows you to cope with challenging situations. It gives you the tenacity and energy, both mental and physical, to continue when you are sure you need to stop. It drives mental perseverance, mental health and supports wellbeing. It is as important to overcoming obstacles in your way as oxygen is to breathing. It is critical in adapting to change.

Tenacity is defined as the ability to become strong, healthy, or successful after experiencing hard or difficult situations. That's a very rudimentary definition, but it's also a very apt one. In short, resilience, underpinned by tenacity, is the ability to bounce back, pick yourself up and keep on going.

Renowned psychologist and educator, Angela Duckworth, calls it something else. She calls it grit. In her words, '*Grit is the secret to outstanding achievement, rather than pure talent. It's not just luck or being in the situation that suits you best. It is a special blend of passion, perseverance and persistence. It is resilience in action. It is grit. And the good news is that this 'grit' can be learned'.*

Like courage, it is not something that all of us are born with. It is something that can be modelled, learned, taught, practised and absorbed.

I am definitely no stranger to resilience, perseverance or grit. I have had to call upon all of them in spades. Through courage and overcoming adversity, my gorgeous girl and I have managed to get to where we are today. Our pathway has led us through tears, through laughter, through difficult times and through fun times. It's been a wild ride, but what has it taught us both? Three words … to be resilient. It has taught us to have grit.

Resilience and grit are often learned in the toughest or worst of situations. But while it's not necessarily imperative to have a world-class disaster for resilience to grow, that's often the quick road to a strong result.

Resilience can grow through commitment to a goal. Grit is made up of the passion and persistence that keep us going towards our goals, working hard to achieve something important to us.

No matter whether these goals are large or small, they can powerfully impact the magnitude of resilience that we grow in the process. Whether that be in large ways or small ways, the ability to bounce back is important in our personal, professional and leadership lives today.

Passing the gift of resilience and grit onto your team is the best legacy you can leave. You can build these traits in yourself and in your teams by understanding strengths. Once you understand your own strengths, and the strengths of the individuals in your team, you need to keep them top of mind.

Another key step in building resilience is building self-esteem. Having confidence in your own abilities and seeing the positive things in life allow you to carry on, even if there are hiccups or missteps along the way.

If you have commitment to a purpose, and have the resilience to see it through, you have all the tools you need to succeed. Right? Well, almost …

People who are resilient and have grit are also flexible. Flexible in the way they think about challenges. Flexible in the way they manage stress.

Flexible leaders are not dependent on one specific style, tactic, or method of leading through adversity. They shift from one strategy to another, depending on the circumstances, and informed through self-awareness and awareness of the demands of their environment. This leadership style requires courage, purpose and clear intention.

Flexible leaders are able to accept what they cannot change, and either work with it or work around it. They also have a growth mindset, being able to take advice and learn from failure. They use emotions and fear to fuel compassion and courage. They turn negative emotions into positive energy to drive teams. They search for opportunities and meaning in adversity.

Entrepreneur and speaker Peter Koerner summed it up so well when he stated: '*Life equals change. So, if you're changing anyway, better or worse are your only choices. Why not change for the better? You can't stay where you are forever.*'

As a leader, what are the practical tools you can use with your teams to help them become resilient and change for the better? There is one tool that is incredibly effective in this space. It's a paradox, an easy but sometimes not-so-easy fix. What is it? It's humour. Yes, humour. And no, I'm not joking.

I love the words of blogger Stacy Brookman when she said: '*Sometimes life is just so screwed up, you have to laugh.*' I don't know about you, there have been in periods in my life where I can definitely relate to this!

I'm not saying you can always laugh your troubles away. Not everything is that simple. But a healthy sense of humour definitely helps in dealing with adversity, in building grit, in building resilience, and in leading with resilience. I've learned this myself and use it as often as I can.

During times of stress and uncertainty, particularly as leaders, it's too easy to inadvertently contribute to a negative situation by taking ourselves too seriously, being in a constantly stressful and reactive mindset, and maybe indulging in self-pity just a little bit too much. As we know, these negative emotions are highly contagious and quickly and easily influence our teams and their performance.

Instead, mentally take a step back, look for any potential humour in the situation and use it to avoid the helplessness that you can get sucked into. It's hard to be a victim when you are laughing. It can also be a survival tactic that is powerfully effective.

Laughter is said to set our spirits free, to clear our heads and restore our sense of balance and purpose. Humour is integral to our peace of mind, mental health and ability to go beyond mere survival. The story of Captain Gerald Coffee, who served in the Vietnam War in the 1970s, illustrates this best.

> Captain Gerald Coffee's story is in equal parts sad, helpless and humorous. The Captain spent seven years as a prisoner of war (POW) in a POW camp in Vietnam. This surely eclipses a lot of the adversities we face in our lives and workplaces today! But the techniques he applied there are relevant still.
>
> During the war, POWs were kept strictly isolated from each other. The theory was that without contact, the prisoner's spirits would soon be broken, and they would be compliant with whatever the enemy needed them to do. But these resilient soldiers did not allow themselves to be broken. They kept their own spirits up by communicating with each other using Morse Code to tap on the walls. They tapped jokes to each other to keep their sanity, their humour and their spirits high. This allowed them some

much needed comedic relief and also some contact with other human beings.

In the grim situation the soldiers were in, sometimes even the comedy became grim, but it still worked for them. One story was that the guards would use ropes to torture the prisoners. When new POWs arrived, the others would very quickly fill them in on the daily routines, how they communicated with each other and what to expect from the guards or prison authorities. When it came to the rope torture, they would be offered the assurance that '*it's really not so bad once you get to know the ropes*'. Yes, it's grim, but it kept them alive and sane.

On a side point for a moment, there has been research that shows that changing the narrative, writing with expression, and communicating your thoughts to others through the physical act of writing, can help greatly in building resilience. This is what Captain Coffee, and his prisoner mates did to survive their horrendous environment.

There is another story from the Captain that underpins this. During his stay in the POW camp, he was moved into a new cell. In the dreary shower area, a previous inmate had scratched into a wall the words 'Smile, you're on candid camera'. It brought a legitimate laugh-out-loud moment to the Captain.

It shows the lasting impact of written communication on resilience. We assume it was a release for the previous inmate, and it was definitely that for the Captain. It also shows the impact of humour. Humour really was the best medicine then, and still is today.

How does a sense of humour support resilience? The health benefits of humour have been well documented. Humour boosts your immune system; it reduces anxiety and stress; it helps to alleviate worry, sadness and guilt; it relaxes muscles, lowers blood pressure, increases pain tolerance and speeds up your body's natural healing process.

Humour is a release of emotions and pain, supporting emotional health and increasing tolerance for difficulties. It helps us to make sense of our situation and cope. Humour does this through improving mood and mental function for you and your team. It's contagious. You can't spend too long with a humorous person without being tickled by one or two pieces of their humour. You may not find all of it helpful, and it might be mostly annoying, but there is likely to be some point that makes you smile at least.

Humour also drives positive behaviour. It means we talk more, make more eye contact with others, touch others and connect. As humans we have an innate need to be connected to others, and humour facilitates this.

As a leader, how can you help your team build an attitude of resilience and display gritty behaviour through humour? Here are some ideas:

- Lead by example and learn to laugh at yourself. If you can laugh at yourself, even if the situation is embarrassing, it will catch on.
- Share funny moments with the team to keep spirits and morale up.
- Seek out playful people who laugh easily to add to your team.
- Use humour and fun as an allure for people to join your team. It will give you a winning edge.
- Find some funny material—cartoons, appropriate jokes, hilarious stories—and share them during tough times.

- Where you can, remove negative influences from your life and from your team. They are not helpful; you don't need them.

A good laugh will not just help your health, allow you to forget about your challenges for a little while, and boost team morale. It will help people align with your purpose and your drive to achieve results, and also bring your teams closer together.

A 2016 study in the journal *Cognitive Processing* shows that researchers in Austria discovered that funny people, particularly those who enjoy dark humour, have higher IQs than their less-funny peers, and learn more easily. Using humour as a source of resilience and a way to help lead your team through adversity and tough times takes courage. It takes purpose. It delivers impact.

It's also about balance and counterbalance. As we have established in the previous chapter, the balance between Yin and Yang in Chinese Taoism is where results are delivered. Two opposites—the negative and the positive, the difficult times and the humorous times—work together to achieve the best result. It's at the junction of these opposites that true value can be realised. It is the juxtaposition of the hard and the soft that builds resilience. One without the other would deliver an unbalanced outcome and limit growth potential, both for your teams and the individuals in them.

Another way to build resilience or grit in your teams is to expand and grow neuroplasticity. Neuroplasticity, also known as brain plasticity, is the ability of our brains to modify their existing connections or re-wire themselves when needed. This is most common in growing children, or in those who have suffered a brain injury. In a work scenario, neuroplasticity can help with retraining or encouraging our brains to adopt new ways of working.

Ultimately, our brains are muscles, with muscle memory, and we can train them to grow and improve. This is the basis of growth mindset. You can train yourself to recognise behaviours that are not helpful and change those behaviours by using self-awareness and mindfulness. A growth mindset of continuously identifying opportunities to improve, and consistently practicing new behaviours, means we can retrain our brains not to shut down in panic and stress.

We can train them to switch on. To become creative. We can manage our responses in crisis situations. We can increase our resilience. We can build our grit. Leading to build resilience, to build grit, takes strength. To lead in this space takes courage. This is courageous leadership exemplified.

States of stress reduce the availability of our cognitive powers, as the brain is otherwise occupied, and overall performance is reduced. Stress actually reduces our neuroplasticity. In this case, resilience to stress and grit in action are critical.

When your team is going through a tough time, when you are striving to overcome obstacles so you can achieve purpose and deliver with impact, when you are leading with courage through adversity and empowering your teams to follow you, resilience is vital to thrive and succeed.

The counterbalance of Yin and Yang; humorous relief through adversity; building neuroplasticity and connections: they all draw teams closer together and allow them to pull together. Humour gives you individual strength, connection and collective strength.

Have the courage to have fun. To build and grow. To laugh.

*'Life shrinks or expands in
proportion to one's courage.'*

ANAIS NIN

Write down 5 insights and actions from this chapter that will help ensure you will act with resilience:

- ....

- ....

- ....

- ....

- ....

Courageous Thoughts

Two key building blocks of resilience that deliver the most impact for the least change and effort are flexibility and humour. Instilling these in your teams will drive positive improvement.

Leading through courage, with balance and purpose, will drive impact and high performance in your teams, building the resilience needed to achieve in the face of challenge.

Most of all, have the courage to have fun. Find the courage to laugh whether it's appropriate or inappropriate, just laugh with your team.

COURAGE IN LIFE

'Do not judge me by my success, judge me by how many times I fell down and got back up again.'

NELSON MANDELA

COURAGE TO CONNECT

'Inaction breeds doubt and fear. Action breeds confidence and courage. If you want to conquer fear, do not sit home and think about it. Go out and get busy.'

DALE CARNEGIE

Remember the story of the martial arts teacher and the student in the introduction to this book? This story was about being curious with others and having the courage to connect. Having a curious mindset means that we have to pay more attention to something, and this impacts our motivation. By taking a courageous step to be more curious, you can build exciting new connections.

In a Harvard Gazette interview with the Dalai Lama, he indicated that '*connection is an answer to global turmoil*'. He emphasised that the potential for happiness is in that connectivity. '*Happiness is in the mind,*' the Dalai Lama said. As individuals and as leaders, when we reach out to others, lifting them up, we experience that connection, and the resulting fulfilment brings us happiness.

In addition, Maxine Harley, psychotherapist poses a question: *Have you ever wondered why there is so much unhappiness, drug abuse, alcoholism and violence in our society?* Might there be one underlying cause for all this dis-ease? Maxine believes it's the result of 'dis-connection' and summarises her thoughts on connection:

- *We crave those connections which enrich us and give us something to smile about. The sort of connections that give us something to live for.*
- *We all have a need to belong somewhere, to feel appreciated and wanted, to feel worthy and worthwhile, and to make a difference.*
- *We all need to feel loved and deserving of compassion, empathy, love and support.*
- *Without meaningful connections we often try to squash or silence that bitter pain of disconnection by being over-busy, over-eating and drinking, gambling, drugs, sex, retail therapy, computer games, pornography—in fact, anything that alters our mood in the short term.*

The Canadian Mental Health Association (CMHA) also refers to the importance of human connection. In today's age, we live busy lives, trying to strike a balance between work, school, hobbies, self-care and often, our social connections fall by the wayside. But connecting with others is more important than you might think.

The CMHA indicates that social connection can lower anxiety and depression, help us regulate our emotions, lead to higher self-esteem and empathy, and improve our immune systems. By neglecting our need to connect, we put our health at risk.

The reality is that we're living in a time of true disconnection as shown by the CMHA. While technology seems to connect us more than ever, the screens around us disconnect us from nature, from ourselves, and from others. Wi-Fi alone isn't enough to fulfil our social needs – we need face-to-face interaction to thrive. Technology should be enhancing our connection to others, not replacing it. If you're feeling lonely, know you're not the only one. And that you don't have to live in isolation. We live in a world with over seven billion people, and we all need connection.

Regarding empathy and leadership, Satya Nadella, the CEO of Microsoft says that if you have empathy for your people, they will do their best work, your team will do their best, and you will make progress.

Adam Grants book *Give and Take*, indicates that for generations we have focused on the individual drivers of success: passion, hard work, talent, and luck. But today, success is increasingly dependent on how we interact with others. It turns out that at work, most people operate as either takers, matchers, or givers. Whereas takers strive to get as much as possible from others and matchers aim to trade evenly, givers are the rare breed of people who contribute to others without expecting anything in return.

In my experience, and as the pressure mounts to be continually innovative in business, leaders are looking for alternative ideas. However, did you know the connections you make with people and your team can be the difference between a good leader and a great one? And, if you build in curiosity as a part of your daily habits, you will always search for more opportunities to connect.

Think about it! A healthy open relationship encourages a productive team. And, while it might sound a little soft from a leadership perspective, today's leaders are still looking for hard outcomes and goals. Many leaders today tend to emphasise their strength and competence but by doing so, they risk alienating through their fear and distrust. Fear can affect creativity and shadow your employees, so they are not working to the best of their ability. Without trust, employees fail to adapt to the values or long-term goals of the overall organisation. Teamwork and bonding can also fall by the wayside.

On the other hand, developing a more collaborative environment, demonstrating openness and encouraging communication at all levels will have the opposite effect. Remember, micro-managing will get you nowhere. Trust needs to be developed over a period of time and while it can be difficult to build, it is necessary to maintain. Trust builds the team up to facilitate a healthy exchange of ideas and acceptance, and it can influence a change in people's attitudes and beliefs.

If you want to cultivate trust, personalise your efforts. Reach out and demonstrate that you, as the leader, are on the same page. If your aim is to have people listen and agree with you, you have to make a concerted effort to listen to and agree with them, where possible. Acknowledge emotions such as fear and tackle any concerns head on.

It is hard to predict how things will change in the future of business, but it is important that we trust the process and focus on a non-traditional mix of employees. Organisations need to seek out individuals who can adapt and collaborate, and in turn be creative and flexible. Diversity will be the key to the future – different backgrounds, different skills – all able to get along and support one another in all organisational endeavours. The future of business is only going to get more interesting. And the relationship between the leader and their team is at the very core.

Connections need to be formed outside of the company as well. Leaders often forget the importance of networking and learning with others; instead, they prefer to focus on competition and strategy. Walls need to come down, and partnerships need to be developed to grow lucrative businesses. Developing relationships with partners can be problematic, but despite the hurdles, the benefits are enormous. Partnering increases the potential for innovation that companies are seeking. So, focus on fostering the relationships between partners, rather than keeping them at arm's length.

Interconnectedness and communication are vital requirements for leaders today, tomorrow and in the future. As Zig Ziglar so beautifully said, '*In many ways, effective communication begins with mutual respect, communication that inspires, and encourages others to do their best.*' And this raises the bar for the organisation as a whole.

The impact of the global pandemic has highlighted the importance of connection with others—taking time to talk to the neighbours, making a call to a friend, caring for a co-worker. Curiosity and connection need to become an ongoing habit, whether in a personal, community or business situation. When we take time to build those connections, we will be rewarded!

And here are some ways to connect through curiosity:

- Ask questions that are not yes/no answers.
- Note what you learn each time in a new situation.
- Listen.
- Be flexible.
- Practise empathy with curiosity.

_____

Write down 5 insights and actions from this chapter to help you increase curiosity and connections:

- ....

- ....

- ....

- ....

- ....

Courageous Thoughts

Leaders who connect inspire their teams to work together to achieve a shared goal through gaining the trust and respect of team members.

Your role as a leader is to create an environment that allows your team to achieve; an environment that is positive, collaborative, inspiring, purpose-driven and empowering.

COURAGE TO BE UNPOPULAR

'The courage to be happy also includes the courage to be unpopular, to be disliked. When you have gained that courage, your interpersonal relationships will all at once change into things of lightness.'

ICHIRO KISHIMI, JAPANESE PHILOSOPHER

L eadership is not always a glamourous job. Let's not be under any illusions here. Being a great leader means hard work. It takes grit. It takes strong resilience when faced with discomfort. It means that sometimes you may become unpopular because of some decisions you make. You may be disliked. The reality of this can be confronting. It's not a comfortable thought at all.

I'm a big fan of the television series, The Office. It's the complexity in its underlying messages, interactions and behaviours that I love. While I have many favourite lines out of the series, one of my favourite quotes from the mockumentary comes from the scene when the regional manager, Michael Scott (played by Steve Carell), is responding to a question about how important it is to him to be liked and to be popular. His answer to his colleague's question is both hilarious and eye opening: '*Do I need to be liked? Absolutely not. I like to be liked. I enjoy being liked. I have to be liked. But it's not like a compulsive need to be liked. Like my need to be praised.*'

This is tongue-in-cheek humour of course, but it highlights a valuable point. Being liked or popular is not a necessity in a leadership setting, but our own emotions may have convinced us that it is. Most of us have a need to be appreciated and praised for what we do, but sometimes we find ourselves in a situation where this is not an option. Sometimes, in making courageous or tough decisions, we will find ourselves without thanks, and low in the popularity stakes.

This popularity game seems to be all too common in the leadership space today. But being popular at all times is not sustainable, and it is a fickle measure of success. Just look at government opinion polls week to week.

As a strong and courageous leader, you are not always going to be popular. Being liked and being popular don't necessarily mean you are respected. On the flipside, being unpopular at times during your leadership career doesn't mean that people will lose respect for you. They may not agree with you or like you, but they may still respect you for your strong actions and meaningful results.

I have an acquaintance whose goal is to always please everyone. In pleasing everyone, he assumes that he will be highly thought of, liked and popular with everyone he comes into contact with. Unfortunately, in his quest to please everyone, he doesn't make hard decisions. He says yes to everyone, and understandably, this inevitably causes everyone involved to be offside. So begins another cycle of behaviour, intended to make everyone happy again, and to return to favour. It's tiring. It's unnecessary. It's not great leadership; it's not even good leadership. It's not positive behaviour.

You can't please everyone all of the time. It's impossible. At some point someone is not going to be pleased and you are not going to be popular.

Often, as you make hard decisions and have tough conversations as a good leader, you will find yourself in unpopular territory. Do you know what? That's okay! That's even good! It's part of courageous leadership and an attribute of a courageous leader—be yourself, authentically and consistently. This earns respect, which is stronger and more enduring. Respect is not reliant on your ratings in the popularity poll. Here's some examples about creating results while being unpopular:

Do you think that former Virgin Australia CEO, Paul Scurrah, was popular for his decision to cut 750 jobs from the organisation in 2019, in his first six months as CEO? Probably not. Was he respected, though, for doing what needed to be done to help the flailing business back to profit? Yes, even by those he was unpopular with.

Once again, following the sale of the Virgin Australia business to Bain Capital, tough decisions had to be made to shore up the business, rescue it from voluntary administration and support its future profitability. The decisions to further cut jobs and reduce the size of the business were also not popular, but the new owners knew they were essential if they were to save the business and make it profitable again.

It takes tough decisions sometimes to bring about the best results. Sometimes courageous leaders can be very unpopular, but in the long run, they can earn respect if they are motivated to do the best they can for others, rather than for their own gain.

So, where does this aversion to being unpopular come from? Simply put, it's part of our nature as humans. We want to belong, and in order to belong, we feel we need to be liked and to fit in with our peer groups. But sometimes we just have to accept that some people won't like us; that we won't always be popular.

To illustrate, let's look at some numbers for a moment. If you are associated with a group of 10 people, statistics say that one person of that 10 will be likely to really like you. That feels good. Until you learn that two people of the 10 will be likely to dislike you. This is a bit uncomfortable. The kicker is that the remaining seven people in the group will be likely to hold a neutral opinion of you. You will be neither popular nor unpopular with them.

These aren't the best odds! Using this theory, we have to accept that at some point in our leadership journey we will be unpopular with more people than we are popular with. And the majority are likely to be neutral about us, so could easily swing either way. If popularity is your goal, your natural anxiety might now flare up, knowing these figures. Working with this takes courage.

Despite these odds, we can't let ourselves be influenced or driven by the often-unpredictable opinions of others. They can change very quickly. We know that political opinion polls can change hourly and would probably change more often if we bothered to measure them more frequently. When an election looms, you have vivid examples of just how unreliable popular opinion is.

Courageous leadership is about making the right decisions for the right reasons, knowing that by doing so, you will contribute to delivering on your long-term purpose. To underpin this, let's borrow from the popular Japanese book, *The Courage to be Disliked*, by Ichiro Kishimi:

'If one really has a feeling of contribution, one will no longer have any need for recognition from others. Because one will already have the real awareness that "I am of use to someone" without needing to go out of one's way to be acknowledged by others. In other words, a person who is obsessed with the desire for recognition does not have any community feeling yet, and has not managed to engage in self-acceptance, confidence in others, or contribution to others.'

These thoughts are sobering. They make a very deep impression on many people. They should have an even deeper impact with leaders, as this is the essence of true courageous leadership.

As leaders, if our sole focus is to be popular, we run a high risk of making bad decisions. We will also be more likely to avoid tough conversations. This is not treating those around us with kindness. It is not showing them the care and respect they deserve. It is not leading with courage. Ultimately, popularity is purely a self-focused goal. It is not selfless—and we know that true courage is. True courage and courageous leadership cannot exist with self-centredness or selfish pursuits.

But be careful. Accepting the idea that at some point we are likely to be unpopular doesn't give us, as leaders, free rein to be or act like jerks. Our goal should not be to purposely make ourselves unpopular! This is also not courageous or kind leadership.

What is the balance then? The answer is that we have to accept that at some point our decisions may mean we are unpopular, and that's okay. The ideal is to be detached from whether or not we are popular, so we are not letting this drive our behaviours or decisions. We must keep in mind that in leading with courage, we must act with kindness and with authenticity, in the best interests of others and our purpose. Balance comes from being guided by our Courage Compass™ rather than an ego-driven self-serving pursuit. Let's reflect on the work of Alfred Adler.

> Adlerian psychology, founded by Alfred Adler, has its foundation in Buddhism and Stoicism. This psychological school of thought teaches understanding of, and appreciation for, the impact and power of cause-and-effect relationships. It proposes that you act and feel a certain way because you choose to, not because your circumstances have driven you to feel that way. It also promotes an understanding that circumstances should not be used to justify your actions, your decisions or your behaviour as a leader.

Adlerian theory continues by suggesting that rather than being popular, as leaders we should focus on self-acceptance, building confidence in others and contribution to others. Adler argues that in combination, these things will reinforce each other in a positive feedback loop. This positive feedback loop, he states, will give you sustainable motivation. It replaces the motivation that is most common; that of being endlessly popular with others.

At this point it's worth reinforcing that courageous leaders are not always unpopular. Don't worry, it's not all doom and gloom. On the contrary, as we discussed, courageous leaders are respected because of their authenticity, their consistency and their high performance. Contribution to others and building confidence in others is their driver. Courageous leadership is their driver, rather than empty social approval.

Let's reflect on more words about courageous leadership:

'As leaders, we should not solely live to satisfy the expectations of others. It is about building a virtuous circle of self-acceptance, building confidence in others and contribution to others.'

ICHIRO KISHIMI

Write down 5 insights and actions from this chapter that reflect your experiences with being popular, and issues with being unpopular:

- ....

- ....

- ....

- ....

- ....

Courageous Thoughts

Leadership is not always a glamourous job. Being
a great leader means hard work. It takes grit. It
takes discomfort. It means that sometimes you
will be disliked for decisions you make.

Being liked in not a necessity; though our own
emotions may have convinced us that it is. Being liked
is a motivation that is not sustainable in leadership.

Be yourself, authentically and consistently. This earns you
respect, which is not reliant on being liked or disliked.

COURAGEOUS HABITS

'Courage, like fear, is a habit. The more you do it, the more you do it, and this habit—of stepping up, of taking action—more than anything else, will move you in a different direction.

— TONY ROBBINS

As a leadership coach, two of the key attributes I work on with leaders are their productivity and their mindset. These are common problems for leaders in many organisations and businesses, compounded by the added challenges of leading remotely and virtually. The rapid pace of change, along with these challenges, have left many executives and leaders struggling to stay organised and focused, resulting in lack-lustre results.

The key to the success of any productivity system is to focus on value, not effort—and this takes courage.

Leaders who focus on checking as many things off their to-do lists as they can each day, without thinking about what they put on those lists, will get a lot done, but often fail to deliver significant results. Leaders who consider what is most important during these times—highest-impact actions—will create long-term value and be exceptionally successful. In turn, it is imperative you review your own mindset and thoughts (and I add techniques to this as well) on how to keep your people productive and positive.

One of the best habits that will help you in this pursuit is to develop a personal weekly planning and mindset process. By taking the time to plan your week, you can identify the best use of your time and energy and organise yourself for success.

Here's how I plan my week on Sunday night so that I can hit the ground running Monday morning with confidence, courage and motivation.

- **Do a mindset map.** The first thing I do anytime I'm thinking about the bigger picture and trying to make a plan is a mindset map. This process walks me through a list of prompts in different categories, looking for things I'm trying to remember and commitments I've made (what scientists call cognitive load), and gets them out onto paper. This gets the distractions out of my head so I can focus better on the work at hand. In turn, I also do a mindset map on things that are disempowering—I ask myself if I have any ANTs (automatic negative thoughts) that are not serving me. If so, I write them down and delete them from my mind. Then I write positive and powerful affirmations—for instance, at present I am writing 'I have got this!' It's vital to have a great mindset.

- **Review the week to come.** My next step is to review the coming week's schedule and look at what I have planned and where I can block time to do my own work, which is important for my long-term goals. In turn, I make sure I have scheduled daily meetings and time to check on my team and team members to make sure I am there for them. It is important during this time to schedule more time in my diary for calls and Zoom meetings (I put my camera on!) to make sure we are all energised and focused on our priorities and goals, as well as sharing something funny or inspirational. If my plan is not well organised, I request changes to free up continuous time in my calendar to create focus and to optimise. I also set up habits in my diary, so I have time for self-development and exercise. I also use my Leadership Planner to help me set up my week and month.
- **Schedule time for the team and myself.** I mentioned above that it is important to schedule more time with your team and for yourself during this time. It is important that you are looking after them and you. An engaged team during these challenging times is a high-performance team!

Every day, I schedule a morning and afternoon call with my team (this depends on the team numbers, so empower your direct reports to do the same). I ask them these questions:

- **Morning** – How are you feeling? What are you focusing on today? How can I help you? What do you need from me today?
- **Afternoon** – How are you feeling? How did you go today? Any learnings, successes and lessons? What are you focusing on tomorrow? How can I help? Thank you for your great work.

I also send my team emails, messages and thank-you cards to tell them how much they mean to me too.

I have now scheduled new and better habits into my day and diary with a real focus on affirmations, visualising, journaling, reading, creative time and exercise. As leaders, we need to put the oxygen masks on ourselves more today than ever. This will serve us well for the future. (I am still working on new habits at wine o'clock, but give me a little more time.)

- **Reflect on the last week/s.** Once I have a good grasp on the week/s, I look back at the last week or two and see if there are any open items or actions from previous events that I may have missed. This often happens. I always look for opportunities to write quick thank-you notes and to confirm any actions or plans coming out of previous meetings. I'll also take this time to reflect on what went well and what didn't, and how I can improve my schedule, mindset and planning going forward.
- **Check longer-term goals.** One thing that helps me move forward is checking and reviewing my long-term goals and objectives. Recently, due to Covid, things have shifted slightly; and for many things have shifted a lot. Based on where I want

to be at the end of each month or even each quarter, which is ideal, I check to see where I need to make progress and set tasks for the coming week/s. One of my long-term goals, for instance, is to write another book which is important to my work. In turn, I'll also reach out to people with whom I need to coordinate or collaborate to schedule time or set up meetings. Don't let these challenging times stop you from achieving or checking your long-term goals—use it for fuel to achieve them!

- **Sort by urgency and impact.** Once I have my tasks, goals and reminders written down, I begin to sort and organise. I'll make notes on them and then sort them by two major criteria. First is urgency, which is how critical the task is to this week. Basically, if I push it off to next week, will it cause problems for me or others? The second criteria is impact, which is how much value this task creates for me in the short and long term. At present I am doing better at being vigilant with what is important, such as my well-being, family, work focus and team, and what is not, such as social media and being worried about what is not in my control.

If I've done things correctly, my schedule and mindset will be where it needs to be so I am the best person I can be, and I will have a plan for how the week will unfold.

I will also have several time blocks for focused work, grouping similar tasks so that I can stay in the same mindset and minimise task-switching, which is vital for the brain.

Of course, life happens, and on Monday morning something unexpected could come up and I'll need to replan everything. And that's fine. I will also be prepared and resilient for things that might not be part of my week or plan. The value of planning is not that a plan will execute perfectly. It's that when it doesn't, you'll understand what's on your plate, what your priorities are, and how you want to re-organise things to stay on plan.

Patrick J. Sweeney II, The Fear Guru, talks about how the minds of the greatest leaders work. He has seen amazing changes when people push out of their comfort zone and discover what's truly holding them back. If you do the same thing, you can live the life of your dreams, but you have to find more fear to get there. The transformation goes way beyond your personal life. Courageous leaders who are more open to risk-taking are significantly more successful than their peers.

Here are five habits that anyone can adopt today to become a better leader, think more creatively, develop a better sense of self and be more likely to have their followers trust and believe in them. (Noticeable results will start to show up after five or six weeks, so stick with it.)

- Scare yourself at least once a week.
- Practise positive self-talk.
- Replace judgment with curiosity.
- Adopt a creator mindset.
- Stress your mind and your body.

These five habits will get you on your way to a life of success, health and happiness. You'll be writing the story of your life from a perspective of strength and opportunity, not from fear.

Also, in *Living the 7 Habits: The Courage to Change*, Dr. Stephen Covey shows how successful people have used these principles to solve problems, overcome obstacles, and change their lives. By showing how real people have used the principles to thrive in a changing world, he provides practical guidance and powerful inspiration to readers searching for a proven framework for living a meaningful life.

Write down 5 insights and actions from this chapter that will help you change your habits:

- ....

- ....

- ....

- ....

- ....

Courageous Thoughts

Leaders with purpose inspire their teams to work together to achieve a shared goal through gaining the trust and respect of team members.

Your role as a leader is to create an environment that allows your team to achieve; an environment that is positive, inspiring, purpose-driven and empowering.

COURAGE TO SPEAK UP

'It took me quite a long time to develop a voice, and now that I have it, I am not going to be silent.'

MADELINE ALBRIGHT

You've probably heard the term '*courageous conversations*' in your business circles (I know I have mentioned tough conversations several times in this book), and you may be wondering just what this phrase means, and how courageous conversations can help you improve your leadership. A courageous conversation happens, essentially, when you take control and carry out a difficult conversation (e.g. about poor performance, and you're scared of not being liked for what you say) with confidence and courage.

Leadership is an attitude, and courage is an extremely important part of that attitude. Bravery is also how you become more resilient: as you tackle more of your fears and worries, you're better equipped to handle them.

When business leaders practise courageous conversations, they reap many benefits—and one of the biggest is increasing their resilience. It's only natural to fear those tough conversations in the workplace (and in life) and avoid them if possible—and if you can't avoid them, you run the risk of not communicating clearly because you don't want to come off as too 'harsh'. There's a difference between being rude and getting across points that may be unpleasant, and leaders must keep this in mind if they're going to have effective conversations about those tricky subjects.

Like it or not, as a leader you'll be having many conversations with many different people in the workplace, and handling the difficult ones is essential to being a great leader.

Whether you fear being accused of bullying, unfair dismissal, legal action or even just being disliked, it's imperative that you become proactive in preparing yourself and developing your communication skills so that you'll be communicating assertively and in a positive manner, to get the positive outcomes necessary.

A courageous conversation entails:

- Delivery of honest feedback
- Building acceptance
- Constructive communication
- Managing emotional and other difficult reactions
- Using a step-by-step framework for tough conversations
- Finding the common ground
- Reaching an agreement and commitment
- Maintenance of relationships after talking about difficult issues.

Working on being able to carry out courageous conversations will empower you to become more resilient; the more you deal with these types of conversations, the better equipped you'll feel and the easier it will be to focus on achieving the right outcomes, instead of worrying about whether your team member will like you after you discuss their need for performance improvement with them.

Managers must take the lead in a conversation to avoid going off track, or miscommunicating. I use an effective technique called 'balancing advocacy and inquiry'. Being a manager means that you're the one who has to have the difficult conversations and being able to brush things off to ensure you get to the desired outcome is vital. This is where courageous conversations come in, as you can find many frameworks to provide you with a step-by-step guide on how to structure these discussions effectively.

If leaders don't articulate the problem well, team members can be left confused, and the issue/s won't get resolved, leading to escalation and unnecessary frustration for all involved.

It's time to be brave and start having those courageous conversations: start being open, transparent and honest, and have the courage to say what needs to be said. You'll become more resilient because of it, and it will have a wonderful effect on your business's performance as well.

You'll gain respect from those around you, and you won't be daunted by the idea of difficult conversations anymore.

———————————————————

Write down 5 insights and actions from this chapter that will help you have more courageous conversations:

- ....

- ....

- ....

- ....

- ....

Courageous Thoughts

Leaders with purpose inspire their teams to work together to achieve a shared goal through gaining the trust and respect of team members.

Your role as a leader is to create an environment that allows your team to achieve; an environment that is positive, inspiring, purpose-driven, and empowering.

COURAGE TO STUFF UP

'Anyone who has never made a mistake has never tried anything new.'

ALBERT EINSTEIN

I n 2020, the Australian bush fires and the global pandemic were heartbreaking, and both demanded true leaders to step up and show courage and strength. We saw key leaders like Shane Fitzsimmons, the NSW Rural Fire Service commissioner, and Daniel Andrews, the Premier of Victoria, display strength daily, but we also saw a plethora of other people on our news screens who were notable during those crises, and not all had the title of leader.

Leadership is not just a title or a role, it's an attitude and a mindset.

True leadership capacities are definitely tested during times of crisis. Leadership, courage, and performance under stress reveal how level-headed a person is. They can also show where weaknesses lie. It is important to always keep your wits about you and stay cool in challenging situations. In turn, emotional intelligence and resilience are critical in times where we need to show great courage.

It is also important to be courageous as a leader when mistakes occur.

Let's look at a few key things that every courageous leader does in times of crisis. These are traits you should also keep in mind when running a business.

Courageous leaders are honest and transparent.
Courageous leaders know that the foundations of leadership are integrity and honesty. They are honest and transparent, regardless of what others might say and think. (These traits do seem to be lacking in some leaders we see in reports in the media today, which undermines our trust in them.) How do you build trust which is EVERYTHING in leadership? Lead by example and be honest.

Courageous leaders don't let their emotions get in the way.

The most important thing to do during a crisis is to maintain an example for your people by keeping cool, calm, and collected, which will allow you to think about the curveballs being thrown your way. This can be challenging, and this is something we often coach our clients to handle. I know when I can feel pressure impacting me, it is important to ask for help, take a breath, and look at the bigger picture. I am also one who embraces vulnerability and at times I am comfortable sharing how I am feeling and where I am at. Remember you are not your emotions.

Courageous leaders are truly brave and face fears.

Many people respond to a crisis by being overwhelmed by stress, which turns to fear. It is easy to be afraid when you have a crisis in your life but if you remain brave, people around you will too, and together a strong team will be able to turn anything around. I know when I feel fear, I embrace it and share with my team that we have got this.

Courageous leaders are accountable for their victories and their losses.

Courageous leaders own up to when they make mistakes. After all, we are all human, and someone who is too proud to admit their own mistake is not likely to be someone that others will follow. Taking responsibility for any actions that you have taken that could have contributed to the crisis will be a good way to prompt the people around you into working on the situation with you wholeheartedly, instead of just because they must. Courageous leaders also don't make excuses!

Courageous leaders don't take failures personally.

By separating your personal feelings from the matter at hand, you are better able to focus on what is happening and take care of it in a manner that is going to be most successful for you and those around you. I find that I learn most when I stuff up, even though it is tough not to take it personally.

Courageous leaders possess positive attitudes from start to finish.
The end of a crisis is not just when you pull yourself out of the muck that it had put you in. The end of a crisis is when those around you have started to recover and are moving on, which might take longer. Keeping a positive attitude and pushing through any challenges will keep morale high, which will put things right back on track in no time at all and will also earn you trust and respect from those around you.

In times of crisis, great leaders are needed.
When we think about examples of great leaders that truly embody leadership, we immediately think of the Jacinda Arderns, the Martin Luther Kings, the Nelson Mandelas, the Rosa Parks of this world; the people who wanted to make a difference in the lives of others, while demonstrating kindness, compassion, courage, and other impressive leadership qualities.

Followers look to see whether a leader is courageous before they'll fully accept that person's leadership. If they see courage, it feels safe to 'sign up'. People need courageous leaders in order to feel there's someone to make the tough calls and to take responsibility for them—they need to know that the buck truly does stop with the leader. With a courageous leader, people feel protected—not that they're helpless, but they know the person in charge really has their back.

Empathy, courage, decisiveness, and the willingness to take action, no matter how hard it may be, are the leadership qualities we all need right now.

Write down 5 insights and actions from this chapter which will help you have the courage to stuff up or face a crisis:

- ....

- ....

- ....

- ....

- ....

Courageous Thoughts

Leaders with purpose inspire their teams to work together to achieve a shared goal through gaining the trust and respect of team members.

Your role as a leader is to create an environment that allows your team to achieve; an environment that is positive, inspiring, purpose-driven, and empowering.

COURAGE FOR TEAMS

'Teamwork is the ability to work together toward a common vision, the ability to direct individual accomplishments toward organizational objectives. It is the fuel that allows common people to attain uncommon results.'

ANDREW CARNEGIE, INDUSTRIALIST AND PHILANTHROPIST

I t's in our evolutionary history … we are social creatures. We live in communities. We have families. And more often than not, we work in teams.

Have you ever done something with a group of people or a team that you never would have done by yourself? I think we can all think of an example or two of this.

When we are part of a great team, we are part of a pack. We know there are others who have our back, who are there to support us when we need it, and who we are there to support too. In a team we can feel encouraged. We know we are cared about. We are working as a collective, combining our strengths to deliver results. This can give us the courage to take on difficult situations together; to conquer hard things as part of a team. It also amplifies the satisfaction we feel when we are finished.

There's nothing like the feeling of achieving something together. Of delivering a result as a collective. There's no doubting the power of a strong team. But this can be taken to a new level by adding courage and courageous leadership into the mix.

Bruce Tuckman (1977), a leading management theorist and former Professor of Educational Psychology, outlined four distinct stages of development for teams: forming, storming, norming and performing. He states that when a team comes together, the members must go through the process of getting to know each other and breaking down individual barriers, before becoming one as a collective and performing at a level not possible as individual people.

But this takes courage. It takes courage to form and work through differences (storming), before achieving a new norm and then performing without limits. It takes a courageous leader to inspire a team, to guide them towards their purpose, to encourage them to deliver with impact—to align their direction and goals with the Courage Compass™.

Courage in teams harnesses the power of the collective. Of diversity. Of complementary strengths. While it's a very simple example, there's an old story of a dew drop that highlights this ideal perfectly. It goes something like this …

It was a lovely crisp spring morning. As the sun was rising, a dew drop was slowly becoming aware of its surroundings. It sat there on a leaf, catching the first rays of the morning sun, and throwing it back out at the world. It glistened, occasionally creating little rainbows if the light hit it at the right angle.

The dew drop was very content in its world and proud of its simplicity, its beauty, the light it could reflect and the colour it could create. It knew its purpose; it was to water the plant. To help it to grow. To deliver impact through helping the plant to flourish and reach its potential. How this purpose was to be achieved, though, was a mystery.

There were other dew drops around it, some on the same leaf and some on other leaves. Some were bigger, some were smaller. But they were all separate and individual, glistening in the sun.

As the morning wore on, the wind began to pick up. As it did, the plant began to sway in the breeze, to move with the wind. The leaf started to tip. Sheer terror gripped the little dew drop as gravity pulled it towards the edge of the leaf. This was definitely outside its safe zone. It was sure this change was not good; it was entering the unknown. Why? Why was this happening? Things had been comfortable. Why did they have to change?

If the dew drop fell off the edge of the leaf, it was certain that it would be smashed into a million pieces on the ground below. It would be the end. It seemed so unfair. It seemed so meaningless. It tried desperately to do whatever it could to cling to the leaf. But then something happened. Fear began to turn into resolve. The drop accepted that change was coming. It must be dealt with. The mystery of how it was going to achieve its purpose would be solved.

And with that, the little dew drop let go. Down, down it fell, towards the ground. It took all the courage it could muster, but it had finally taken the plunge into change.

Something was different though. The little dew drop had not expected this. Below there seemed to be a mirror. The little dew drop saw a reflection of itself that seemed to be coming up to meet it. Closer and closer they came together, until the tiny dew drop became part of a pond. Now the dew drop was no more, but it was not destroyed. It became part of a larger whole. It became part of a team that was stronger with numbers. That could deliver infinitely more results than the single little drop could on its own. It took courage to let go and drop into the unknown, but its purpose seemed more achievable and the impact it could deliver was now so much greater.

It might be a simple story, but there is a moral to it. Not one of us is bigger than all of us. As leaders, it's our role to build teams that find joy in being together. Teams who work hard together, who laugh together, who have fun together, work collaboratively as a group and build on the strengths of the individuals. They do not work in silos or in isolation from others in the team or organisation.

In a strong team, together we become so much more than we ever could alone. The little dew drop, with its purpose of watering the plant and helping it to grow, was far more impactful as part of a collective rather than as an individual. It could support a garden to flourish, rather than just one plant.

Great leaders, such as Jeff Bezos of Amazon and Christine Lagarde of the International Monetary Fund, understand the power of the collective, of a team over individuals.

Amazon harnesses the power of crowd sourcing—the power of the collective—to continuously improve their services. It also provides a platform for multiple sellers, so they can attract a larger number of clients than any could on their own. These clients are ready to spend, ready to get a great deal, and ready to shop around on the platform to achieve that.

As a first mover in the market in this space, it took courage for the Amazon team to take a risk on this new, unknown business model. The goal was to bring together resources from around the globe to deliver services and continuously improve the platform and products for customers. In addition, the Amazon team is known for their relaxed, fun culture that really harnesses and builds on the strength of individuals and delivers through the power of a team.

The International Monetary Fund also uses the power of the collective, the power of its members, to deliver international financial stability. Through this collective power, sustainable economic growth and a reduction in global poverty are goals that are quickly being realised. It takes courageous leadership to guide a diverse team, a team that is there for a common purpose, driven to help those around them, acting with courage to deliver impact and results in developing and emerging countries.

Courageous leadership is the essential ingredient when combining individual talents and accomplishments, and directing them towards organisational objectives through teamwork, where people are working together toward a common vision.

Aligning the power of a team with the power of the Courage Compass™ is what courageous leadership is all about. It is how results are delivered. In this environment, teams are built on courage and kindness; they deliver with purpose and are resilient. Leaders lead with courage, with kindness, with purpose and with resilience. This is the fuel that allows common people to attain uncommon results through collaboration. In partnership.

It takes courage to give up your individual agendas and goals, to form and storm with a group. It takes courageous leadership to guide the norming and deliver the performing.

Write down 5 insights and actions from this chapter that relate to or can improve your team experiences:

- ....

- ....

- ....

- ....

- ....

Courageous Thoughts

When we are part of a great team, we are part of a pack.
This can give us the courage to take on difficult situations
together. To conquer hard things as part of a team.

Aligning the power of a team with the power of the
Courage Compass™ is courageous leadership. This is the
fuel that allows common people to attain uncommon
results through collaboration and partnerships.

COURAGE FOR FAMILIES

'The most overwhelming key to a child's success is the positive involvement of parents.'

JANE D. HULL, EDUCATOR AND POLITICIAN

I t's a strange thought. In our urban culture today, we seem keen to segment our lives. Work life is separated from home life. Home life is separated from our social lives. We can feel and act like different people in each. Different versions of ourselves. And we can feel success when none of these worlds collide.

What if these different worlds could work together to improve each other? What would our world be like if we allowed some of these worlds to cross? What would happen if we allowed some of the care we have for our children to show in our engagements as leaders, in our teams at work?

And what if we allowed the courageous leadership we display and encourage in our workplaces to inspire our children to become courageous, brave, and resilient adults? Really, isn't parenting the most important leadership role we will ever face?

What our world needs more of today is courageous parenting—parents who are committed to growing kind, resilient young people. Young people with purpose, who deliver impact.

Parents are leaders. The incredibly courageous parents in the world, like Tame Okada and the parents of Rhuksana Kausar, spread ripples of impact that may be felt for generations to come.

In my role as a parent, I do all I can to lead my daughter with courage and kindness, and to encourage her to be brave—to follow my example as I lead by example. I wrote my book *Just Rock It!* to encourage and support my girl to overcome her self-doubt, her fear, her hesitation; to help her become brave and take on the world with confidence and courage. This is my greatest role in leadership. My role as a mum.

I wanted to give Abby the gift of a set of practical tools and strategies to help her see and realise her inner greatness. To achieve her dreams. That book was also written to help others in the same way—others who might be lacking confidence and limiting themselves with their own thoughts and self-doubts. It was my goal to encourage them to *Just Rock It* in life.

In a business context, the actions and behaviours of good parents can provide a lot of inspiration to turn good leaders into great leaders; while good leaders at work shouldn't hesitate to use their innate leadership skills at home as well, to become great parents. It's a Yin Yang thing again: the confluence of work and home is where the value lies.

A group of psychologists from the University of British Columbia, Queen's University (Canada) and the University of Victoria (Australia) draw a very interesting link between transformational leadership and transformational parenting. The results are particularly powerful for teenagers.

The group proposes that the skills you learn in an MBA could be very helpful in personal situations also, slightly blurring the line between how you as a professional conduct yourself and build value, and how you as a parent conduct yourself and build value.

What does transformational leadership mean in this context? It's the form of leadership that elevates the beliefs and motives of others and supports them in developing and growing.

Transformational leadership and transformational parenting help to develop strong values and purpose, which are incredibly important in both teams and families. It helps in building individual identities in both team members and in children. It is about empowering and encouraging autonomy and responsibility.

Our kids, in particular, can thrive in a transformational leadership environment. They become self-sufficient, confident, and motivated to keep improving themselves. To take on a growth mindset. It also means that both children and parents grow, develop, and continually improve.

What steps can you take in either a business or personal context to realise the benefits of courageous and transformational leadership and parenting? Here's some thoughts:

- A transformational approach means assessing your own feelings and reactions when making decisions.
- Once you have assessed these decisions, it means taking responsibility for your own actions and behaviours. Through leading by example, your teams or teens are more inclined to see the benefits and follow your example.
- Blur the lines between the personal you and the professional you. Show your team you care, in a similar way that you show your children you care. Genuinely caring and being kind can motivate your teams to be more successful, to perform better.
- Listen to your teams and your children; listen like they are the only thing that really matters to you at that time. Don't reschedule one-on-one meetings. Take the time to really connect on what is important to either your team member or your child. They are your top priority in that moment.
- Whether it's your child, your emerging leader, or a team member, create a safe environment for them to try, fail fast and learn.

- Acknowledge mistakes but focus on learning from them rather than punishing them.
- Positive reinforcement is key. Focus on identifying successes, even small ones, and learning from both these and the things that didn't go so right.
- Provide formal and informal coaching, helping to set them up for future challenges that will definitely come, either in a professional or personal environment.
- Make your young ones or your team members feel confident. Their work environment or their home environment is a no-judgement, no-criticism space. It is about constructive discussions that build confidence and guide in the right direction, celebrating all achievements. Confident people outperform insecure people in almost every situation.
- Focus on strengthening strengths. It seems counter intuitive, I know: if it's a strength, why would you focus on this? Wouldn't you be better to place that focus on a weakness that needs work? While this might be useful in some situations, there's a school of thought that if you are looking to build motivation and see fast benefits from quick wins, you should focus on strengthening your strengths, or encouraging your teens or teams to do this. There is already a natural interest in this area, so why not exploit it?
- Believe in those you are leading. Even if they don't necessarily believe in themselves at the beginning, your belief in them can be contagious. In my earlier story of my schoolteacher, his belief in me was contagious. It led to me believing in myself. If you have confidence in your team member or child, that will drive positive behaviours and resilience in them, which help them work through problems and achieve solutions. It's all about showing unwavering belief and support.

- Focus on development. As both a good parent and a good leader, our focus is on developing others. Showing your kids how to wash the dishes properly, then stepping back and letting them do it on their own, is developing them. Yes, it's painful sometimes, and there may be a need to quality check and re-do every now and then. But they quickly improve. It's the same with your teams. Don't rush to jump in and provide a solution. Ask the right questions and be a sounding board to help your team member develop a solution to a situation for themselves.

What are some tools you can use to build your teams and see results with parenting? It's been proven by psychologists, such as the renowned Dr Pamela Rutledge, PhD, MBA, that storytelling is the most effective tool you can use when striving to be a great leader and a great parent.

How does this work regarding creating courageous kids? Your eight-year-old is struggling with her maths homework. She can't grasp the concept, and it's frustratingly just out of her reach. The theory means nothing to her, so her brain just shuts off as soon as it's mentioned. How can you help her understand? You build a story around it. You can be as creative as you like, getting her involved and encouraging her to add to the story. You still guide the conversation to make sure the required lessons are included and learned. And before you know it, she has found the answers she needs through the story. Here's a story to emphasise the point about stories:

The Australian Aboriginal Dreamtime illustrates the power of story. The Dreamtime is the term that describes the unique stories and beliefs which form the glue that holds the Indigenous culture together, and each generation adds to it with their own chapters and embellishments. Elders, parents, and grandparents all tell the same stories to younger generations, passing on knowledge, lessons, and answers to tricky questions that are commonly asked.

Storytelling has also been linked to resilience in general, and more particularly in children. Telling your children stories of your life, of their grandparents, of their history—like the Indigenous Dreamtime stories—gives youngsters a sense of family, a sense of safety and belonging, a sense of pride. It's been proven that people who know their family history and the stories from it have a higher sense of control over their lives. They have higher self-esteem and resilience. Isn't this the role of a leader? To build up your teams? To help your children grow?

Stories of family history, or history of an organisation or a team, help the members understand that others have experienced good and bad, and easy and difficult times before them. And they have made it through.

Storytelling helps build an understanding of how a family or a team has changed, developed, and grown in good times and bad. It's about sharing the lessons that have been learned.

Storytelling helps you set expectations in a more informal situation and drive home the values you would like the listeners to live by. But also keep in mind, this means you need to lead by example and live up to these expectations yourself. Children, in particular, have a very strong sixth sense for spotting double standards and, generally, are only too happy to point them out!

Storytelling is also a great time to introduce some humour and fun. This shows that even in tough times you can laugh, and it teaches our young ones that we shouldn't take ourselves too seriously. Showing them that it is healthy to have a laugh at yourself or your own silly mistakes is a good thing. Lead by example by using your own stories to show that in hindsight things can become very funny, even if they weren't funny in the moment.

People tend to live up to the expectations of their leaders. If you, as either a parent or a leader, believe in those you lead, they will perform better and deliver on that expectation. Our kiddies will perform better with your unwavering belief in them.

If your young one is not performing to the level they are capable of in a particular area of their life, you need to have an honest, caring conversation with them. With kindness, highlight the areas that could be problem areas or improvement opportunities, and encourage them to talk with you about them. These courageous conversations will provide a learning opportunity for you as a leader and for your youngster. It is courageous leadership guided by your own Courage Compass™.

Whether you are a leader in a professional setting or a parent figure, your Courage Compass™ can guide you. It's about leading with courage and leading by example. It's about continually moving forward, no matter what is in your way or blocking you. Together you will find a way around it. It's about instilling this in your family and in your teams.

And remember to always stay kind to yourself. Especially when things are challenging.

'If you can't fly, then run. If you can't run, then walk. If you can't walk, then crawl. But whatever you do, you have to keep moving forward.'

MARTIN LUTHER KING, JR., ACTIVIST, AND MINISTER

———————————————

Write down 5 insights and actions from this chapter about what you could do to create courage in children:

- ....

- ....

- ....

- ....

- ....

Courageous Thoughts

Courageous leadership also extends to our most important leadership role as parents. In a business context, the actions and behaviours of good parents can provide a lot of inspiration to turn good leaders into great leaders. Great leaders at work shouldn't hesitate to use their fine leadership skills at home as well.

LEADERSHIP FOR THE FUTURE

*A leader is one who knows
the way, goes the way,
and shows the way.*

JOHN MAXWELL

COMMIT TO COURAGE

'The most courageous act is still to think for yourself. Aloud.'

COCO CHANEL

When we think of courageous leadership, we often think of people working in emergency services, the army, the police force, fire services, medical units—those people who are on the front lines and making a visible difference in our communities, leading efforts in disasters and catastrophes. Yes, these are very courageous people. Our communities could not function properly without them. They are committed to service and the communities they serve. They lead and serve with purpose and kindness. They lead and serve with resilience. They lead and serve with impact. There is no denying this at all. They are definitely heroes of our communities.

What about those of us who are not involved in these types of activities in our communities? What if this type of courageous leadership is not a part of our normal everyday life? Or can it be? Can we all practise courageous leadership in every aspect of our lives?

It seems much of the world sees courageous leadership as something that only applies to those who risk their lives in the course of their jobs. Yes, those roles do require bravery under very challenging and often life-threatening circumstances. But that is not the full extent of courage. That is not courage in its entirety. True courage and courageous leadership are wider, broader, and deeper than this. Courage and courageous leadership can and should be a part of our day-to-day lives. We should be continually guided by our Courage Compass™.

As a courageous leader, you must commit to courage.

Courageous leaders can be found anywhere, at any time. It could be you. Courageous leadership is in all of us. Johan Wolfgang von

Goethe mused that it is '*the commitment to begin, without any guarantee of success*' that demonstrates courage.

Courageous leadership is the willingness to tackle difficult challenges, tasks, or issues, whether popular or not. Courageous leaders take complex problems head on, regardless of a lack of a guaranteed outcome. Courageous leaders address difficult topics with their teams, with kindness. They display the ability to take on difficult people, have difficult conversations and help guide teams through difficult journeys.

Where is commitment to courage most evident? Courage is shown in the leader who willingly, tactfully, and kindly addresses the elephant in the room. Who cleverly facilitates a conversation to bring conflict out in the open and move it towards a resolution. Who stimulates healthy discussion, not shying away from diversity of opinion, but recognising the value of courage.

Courage is the leader who is flexible and able to change tack when the situation demands it. Courageous leaders are those who recognise they are also on a learning pathway themselves. On a growth journey. They seek feedback, no matter how uncomfortable, in the pursuit of development. They find their own weak spots and work to improve them. They lead by example, encouraging their teams to follow on the same journey.

Courageous leaders admit and acknowledge their failures, learn from them, and move forward with no loss of momentum or enthusiasm.

It may not be glamourous. It may be a slog some days. It may require baby steps that seem to be taking you nowhere, however it's a little further each day! Sometimes success is a big bang, short-term deliverable. Sometimes it takes a long-term approach, with a series of small things falling into place; small actions with seemingly insignificant results that come together as a cumulative to deliver a transformation. This is leading with courage.

Committing to courage is the starting point. It's not the easily won 'leader lottery' that makes you a millionaire overnight when you deliver results that matter. It's not the get-rich-quick version of a leadership journey. It's about setting a purpose and truly committing to delivering it.

Eleanor Roosevelt, in her powerful 1960 work, *You Learn by Living*, beautifully and theatrically outlined the crux of commitment to courage and its opportunity:

> 'The encouraging thing is that every time you meet a situation, though you may think at the time it is an impossibility, and you go through the tortures of the damned, once you have met it and lived through it you find that forever after you are freer than you ever were before. If you can live through that you can live through anything. You gain strength, courage, and confidence by every experience in which you stop to look fear in the face. You are able to say to yourself, "I lived through this horror. I can take the next thing that comes along." The danger lies in refusing to face the fear, in not daring to come to grips with it. If you fail anywhere along this line, it will take away your confidence. You must make yourself succeed every time. You must do the thing you think you cannot do.'

Courageous leaders are servant leaders. They are externally focused; they lead by example. They demonstrate and display the behaviours that will drive development in their teams, that will drive the performance of the business.

A courageous path takes purpose and a pledge, committing to using the Courage Compass™ to guide you as a leader, committing to leading by example with kindness and flexibility. This means keeping your eye on your goal and being guided by your compass. There's no guarantee of success; but a guarantee to do what needs to be done, regardless of the adversity and the outcome, will drive success in the long term. This 'success' may be a positive result, or success in learning from setbacks or seeming failures. It's a commitment to a continuing growth mindset, learning, developing, and expanding. This is courageous leadership.

'Commitment is what transforms a promise into a reality.'

ABRAHAM LINCOLN, 16TH PRESIDENT OF THE UNITED STATES OF AMERICA

———————————————————

Write down 5 insights and actions for you from this chapter about how you will commit to courage:

- • ....
- • ....
- • ....
- • ....
- • ....

Courageous Thoughts

Courageous leaders can be found anywhere and
anytime. It could be you. Courageous leadership
is in all of us. It takes commitment to bring it
to the forefront and realise it's true power.

Courageous leaders admit and acknowledge their
failures, learn from them, and move forward
with no loss of momentum or enthusiasm.

COURAGE PLEDGE

'A lot of people are afraid
to say what they want.
That's why they don't
get what they want.'

MADONNA

Today's world is complex. We face multi-faceted issues and complex problems daily. Leaders must move with speed, leading teams through both good times and bad, working through mind-boggling complexity, and delivering resourceful solutions. There is often no reliable map showing the way, so we must use our purpose, goals, and direction to guide us.

I am regularly exasperated by my car's GPS when the new roads that have been built have not been mapped yet, or my system is missing the latest update. On a recent expedition my GPS told me that I was driving through an open paddock, when in reality I was driving on a shiny new six-lane motorway. I knew I was heading the wrong way, but there was no way to turn around. My GPS had no idea where I was … it was honestly infuriating, and I was feeling a whole new level of helplessness and anxiety. I had to rely solely on my sense of direction to guide me.

After quite a few choice words to the GPS, I used an emergency turn-around lane (I promise I won't do it often) and got myself back on track purely by maintaining my sense of direction. It took commitment. Occasionally it meant ignoring what seemed to be my better judgement in favour of my intuition. But I knew the way I needed to head, and finally found the road I needed to be on to get there.

My sense of direction saved me. My sense of true north. As leaders we need a compass to help us keep heading on the right course when our GPS is wrong, our maps are not current, or when roads have been moved. We need this tool to guide us on the right path, giving us the flexibility to move around obstacles in our way, to change roads and take the occasional detour, while still maintaining our course.

It might take some creativity, but in the leadership space we need to commit to navigating unchartered territory and off-roading, if necessary, in order to follow the right direction. It's not always a comfortable behaviour. It's not always easy. It might not be popular, and it might mean you, as a leader, are disliked. That's all okay. As a courageous leader, you just need to be committed.

We need to commit to courage. We need to commit to courageous leadership. We need to pledge ourselves to be servant leaders, to have a growth mindset, to lead with kindness, resilience, purpose, and impact.

As courageous leaders we promise:

- Kindness over heartlessness or mercilessness
- Purpose over lack of direction
- Resilience over weakness and wavering
- Impact over non-delivery
- Creativity over compliance
- Diversity over conformance
- Empowerment over control
- Thinking over following
- Flexibility over stubborn rigidity
- Leading with a compass instead of a map

At the centre of your compass is you. You need to be the change. If you are leading with courage, using your Courage Compass™ with authenticity, you will be successful.

The north point on your compass represents influencing up in your organisation, influencing those above you.

East and west represent leading and supporting your colleagues and peers, creating win-win situations.

The south point represents your impact flowing down to those in your teams and leading by example.

I respect ancient Roman philosopher, Seneca's words in saying that '*there is nothing in the world so much admired as a man or woman* (in our context, a leader) *who knows how to bear adversity with courage*'.

To continue this journey, as leaders, we must commit ourselves. Pledge to start a lasting change in our world, in our teams. Be courageous in the face of adversity. Use kindness and strength at every point possible. Lead with purpose and with resilience. Deliver impacts that positively change the world around us. Set the example for people to follow.

Embark on this journey with me now. This is our courageous pledge.

'To embark on the journey towards your goals and dreams requires bravery. To remain on that path requires courage. The bridge that merges the two is commitment.'

STEVE MARABOLI, WRITER

Write down 5 insights and actions from this chapter about your pledge to courage:

- ....

- ....

- ....

- ....

- ....

Courageous Thoughts

Use your Courage Compass™ to manage upwards and outwards, while cascading positive impact to your teams.

You are the centre of your compass.
You need to be the change you want to see.

Pledge to lead with kindness, with purpose,
with impact, with resilience. Pledge to lead
with your Courage Compass™.

THE COURAGEOUS PLAN

*'Plan your work and
work your plan.'*

NAPOLEAN HILL

The year of 2020 brought world-changing events, so it provided an excellent opportunity to reflect, review and decide how coming years will be different for you. You may have already considered your own personal preferences, however as a leader, where would you like to make an impact this year and beyond?

Let's explore leadership planning. Knowing where to start your leadership journey requires you to be very clear on past leadership outcomes: your performance, your successes, and what you could do differently. Then, by noticing trends and where you can meet the gaps, you can establish your own leadership plan!

Your success in leadership and business is your own hands: enjoy the discovery process! As John F. Kennedy once said, '*Leadership and learning are indispensable to each other*'.

Every day is a powerful day and guess who holds the power? YOU! As you may know, I am obsessed with neuroscience and I state this frequently: '*Where attention goes, energy flows and courage builds.*' Remember, you are the director of your mind and thoughts, and I want everyone to have powerful and courageous thoughts for a focus this year and every year.

When I was writing and publishing this book, *First Comes Courage*, during COVID, I didn't know if I had it in me to complete it. Like many of you, I too experienced a year of many ups and downs in 2020, however I knew I had to set my intention to be courageous, as this is what I stand for and encapsulates the impact I want to make.

If you have disempowering and fearful thoughts, and you focus on those, you will have a negative movie showing to the world. If you embrace the fear, this will drive courage and action. The mind is a powerful thing and the more you focus on something, the more you will see the data and evidence that supports it. Set your focus and intention to being courageous and being the best version of you.

Because better questions give better answers, here are five powerful questions to ask yourself EVERYDAY:

- What do I really want and why?
- Who do I want and choose to be and why?
- What is stopping me from being who I am and getting what I want?
- What are my intentions and where will my focus be today?
- What action/s can I do today to be courageous (no matter how small)?

Underpinning all of our courageous behaviour is KINDNESS. Remember to be kind to yourself and others. Focus on who you are, what you want, and what makes you rock. Yes, leadership is about how we can be kind and help others, however, don't compare yourself and your inner courage and successes with others.

'The first step to getting what you want is to have the courage to get rid of what you don't.'

ZIG ZIGLAR

Self-awareness and intention will help you not only find your courage and leadership capabilities—you will also find your purpose and impact as a person and leader.

Always reflect on your day and celebrate the small wins, successes, and achievements. If you had a day of NON-courage or UN-kindness for yourself, then laugh at it and learn from it.

Maureen Metcalf, from the Forbes Coaches Council outlines 'Leadership Trends for 2021 And Beyond'. She says that where there is disruption, there is an opportunity. Where there is a collapse, there is an evolutionary opportunity. As an interconnected global system, we are facing opportunities to address risks and create a more sustainable, just and fair future for more people. To create this future, leaders need to understand the current leadership trends as well as the overarching megatrends, which are:

> **Trend 1:** Economic volatility impacting society and the workplace, increasing polarisation on global sustainability, and social justice issues impacting international relations and local communities.
> **Trend 2:** Continued erosion of trust in societal institutions and a weakening of the principles that sustain those institutions.
> **Trend 3:** More complex global system optimisation, including resilience, geopolitical impacts, social justice, etc.
> **Trend 4:** Increased expectations to deliver results faster.
> **Trend 5:** Major shift in knowledge and skill requirements for both leaders and employees
> **Trend 6:** Need to increase personal agility in all facets of life.
> **Trend 7:** More freedom to work where and how we want—and less privacy.

We are living at a fantastic time in history. We have the opportunity to plot a future that is unlike our past. We can leave a legacy where future generations look back and see this time as a renaissance—*when the foundation was laid to create a future better than many people living could imagine.* A future where all of the world's population has enough food and water. A future where human exploitation is an exception rather than a common occurrence. A future where people earn a living wage to provide for their families without relying on government assistance. A future where organisations balance robust financial rewards with creating healthier communities and societies.

We have the power to make progress to co-create the future we envision—whatever that future is. I invite you to imagine the impact you want to see, and work to create it.

———————————————————

Write down 5 insights and actions from this chapter that will help you plan with courage:

- ....

- ....

- ....

- ....

- ....

Courageous Thoughts

Leaders with purpose inspire their teams to work
together to achieve a shared goal through gaining
the trust and respect of team members.

Your role as a leader is to create an environment that
allows your team to achieve; an environment that is
positive, inspiring, purpose-driven, and empowering.

CHAPTER TWENTY-ONE

FINAL COURAGEOUS THOUGHTS

'Success is not final; failure is not fatal: it is the courage to continue that counts.'

WINSTON S. CHURCHILL, STATESMAN AND WRITER

There will be times in our professional lives and our personal lives where everything goes to plan. We are on track, we are kicking goals, everything seems sunny, and the future seems bright.

Then there will be times when we seem to lose our focus. We lose our direction. We can't see the forest for the trees, and we can't see past the next hour, the next disaster. We've all been in this space at some point in our lives. We all know that harrowing feeling of being out of control—these challenging times can lead the strongest of people to the brink of despair.

I have experienced these dark times in my life, during my experience in China and in the tough times I have been through with Abby, my daughter. These were times of fear. Times of tears. All seemed hopeless.

At such times we need something outside ourselves to guide us. We need something reliable. Something of value that has never let us down.

At these times we need a goal to focus on, even if it is just to make it through the next hour or the next day. And in pursuit of our goal, we need our Courage Compass™ to guide us. To find the grit to pick ourselves up. To keep going with resilience. To continue to be kind to ourselves and those around us. To embrace fear and use it as motivation to drive change.

It is in these times that we all need to become leaders. Not leaders with all the bells and whistles and trappings of leadership, but true leaders. Leaders who are not always recognised, but who have a real, tangible, and powerful impact on those around us and those who are following us.

Use the power of courage and kindness, of resilience and grit to ultimately deliver with purpose and with impact and pull yourself and those around you through to reach calmer times and brighter days.

'You can be strong as a leader and be kind.

You can be courageous as a leader and be fearful.

You can be a leader without the title.

But first comes courage.'

SONIA MCDONALD

Write down 5 final insights and actions from this book to summarise what you have learnt over this journey:

- ● ....

- ● ....

- ● ....

- ● ....

- ● ....

Courageous Thoughts

Leaders with purpose inspire their teams to work together to achieve a shared goal through gaining the trust and respect of team members.

Your role as a leader is to create an environment that allows your team to achieve; an environment that is positive, inspiring, purpose-driven, and empowering.

COURAGEOUS RESOURCES

leadershiphq.com.au

The greatest edge is your leadership and culture. Discover the wide range of services we offer, including leadership assessments and diagnostics, leadership development programs, executive coaching, cultural transformation workshops, online resources, blogs and memberships. Our team members are experts in delivering workshops, programs and coaching in all aspects of leadership. From online, face to face or blended, we work with Executives, Middle Management, Emerging as well as Frontline Leaders.

mcdonaldinc.com.au

We specialise in connecting organisations and talent through recruitment services and provide human resources consulting. The core to our recruitment process is ensuring that your values align with the values of the candidates we submit to you. Once we find your talent, we engage a transition coach to ensure that the first 90 days of transition are smooth and successful for you, their direct manager, and the talent.

soniamcdonald.com.au

Author, international keynote speaker, and advisor, Sonia inspires and creates great leaders, teams, and companies across the globe. Make your next event outstanding, with Sonia's high energy, inspirational and relatable keynotes, packed full of actionable advice. Delivered virtually or in-person.

outstandingleadershipawards.com.au

Annual Global Leadership Awards Ceremony that recognises leaders, teams and companies that espouse courage, kindness, inclusivity, and authenticity.

'Leadership Attitude'

The first on Sonia's books explores how mindset and action can change your world. The way you lead. Your results. Choosing your leadership attitude can influence your leadership style, your effectiveness, and your success.

'Just Rock It!'

Sonia's second book is a book of action. It's a book of change. It's a book of strategies, pieces of wisdom and endless encouragement to help you break through your fear. Stop doubting yourself. Stop making excuses. Set your vision and set yourself to achieve it.

WHAT'S NEXT?

Sonia's mission in life is to help people become their very best selves. If you want to start taking actionable steps on your leadership journey, here is where to begin.

The Leadership Lab
An Online Membership that contains great tools for leaders to develop their skills, including masterclasses, leadership interviews, books, article library, discounts to events and much more. sonia-mcdonald. mykajabi.com/lab

Your Leadership Coach Podcast
Sonia's podcasts are fun, inspirational, relatable and packed full of actionable and practical advice to help you uncover your greatness. Sonia's experience, knowledge and passion will leave you empowered and courageous. soundcloud.com/yourleadershipcoach

Courage Compass Leadership Assessment
Provided by LeadershipHQ, this assessment will uncover your strengths and areas for improvement under the four umbrellas of courage: Kindness, Impact, Purpose and Resilience

Public Workshops and Events

LeadershipHQ hosts regular high-impact online and in-person public workshops and events to help build a world with greater leaders. leadershiphq.com.au/events/

LeadershipHQ blogs

Our award-winning blogs explore all areas of leadership in small, actionable, and digestible reads. https://leadershiphq.com.au/our-blog-2/

Sonia McDonald blogs

Sonia's blogs are about bringing out the best in you. "I want everyone to be the best versions of themselves and to see and find the greatness, courage and kindness within."
https://soniamcdonald.com.au/blog/

Contact Sonia and the team at:
hello@leadershiphq.com.au
letschat@mcdonaldinc.com.au
sonia@soniamcdonald.com.au

BIBLIOGRAPHY

Adler, A. (1992). *Alfred Adler: Theory and Application.*
www.alfredadler.edu/about/alfred-adler-theory-application

Bloom, A. (2015). For the McKinsey, Stanford, and London School of Economics. Quoted in *The Growing Correlation between Kindness and your Bottom-line.* www.whatsyourkind.com/blog/2016/2/18/the-growing-correlation-between-kindness-and-your-bottom-line

Brookman, Stacey. (n.d.). *Laugh at the Fear: Writing Tough Times With Powerful Humor.* www.stacybrookman.com/laugh-fear-writing-tough-times-powerful-humor/

David, Susan. TED Talk. *The Gift and Power of Emotional Courage.* 2020 www.ideas.ted.com/how-to-be-kinder-to-yourself-self-compassion/

Intelligence and Sense of Humour. Exploring Your Mind. Not Credited. (2018). www.exploringyourmind.com/intelligence-sense-of-humor/

Kishimi, I. and Koga, F. (2018). *The Courage to be Disliked.* Atria Books.

Koerner, Peter. (n.d.). Quoted in www.performancemarks.com/tag/resilience/

Krapivin, P. (2018). *How Google's Strategy For Happy Employees Boosts Its Bottom Line.* Forbes. www.forbes.com/sites/pavelkrapivin/2018/09/17/how-googles-strategy-for-happy-employees-boosts-its-bottom-line/#436d3f1522fc

Marks, Judy. (n.d.). Quoted in Gorman, P. (2018) *Otis Elevator's Judy Marks Talks Leadership, The Future of Manufacturing.* Chief Executive magazine. www.chiefexecutive.net/otis-elevators-judy-marks-talks-leadership-the-future-of-manufacturing/

Morton, K. Barling, J. Rhodes, R. Mâsse, L. Zumbo, B. and Beauchamp, M. (2010). *Extending Transformational Leadership Theory to Parenting and Adolescent Health Behaviours: An Integrative and Theoretical Review.* Health Psychology Review, 4: 2, First published on 29 July 2010.

Oswald, A. Proto, E. and Sgroi, D. (2019). *Happiness and Productivity.* University of Warwick. www.warwick.ac.uk/newsandevents/pressreleases/new_study_shows/

Roosevelt, E. (1960). *You Learn by Living.* Republished, 2009 by Westminster John Knox Press.

Rutledge, P. (2011). *The Psychological Power of Storytelling.* Psychology Today. www.psychologytoday.com/au/blog/positively-media/201101/the-psychological-power-storytelling

Seppala, E. (2013). *Why Compassion in Business Makes Sense.* Greater Good Science Centre. Berkley University.

Tuckman, B. and Jensen, M. (1977). *Stages of Small-Group Development Revisited.* Group and Organization Management, 2(4), pp.419-427.

NOTES

CPSIA information can be obtained
at www.ICGtesting.com
Printed in the USA
LVHW021224280423
745515LV00004B/441